God's Plan of Salvation

The Journey from Hearing to Holy Living

James Majors

God's Plan of Salvation: The Journey from Hearing to Holy Living

Copyright © 2026 James Majors

All rights reserved. No part of this publication may be reproduced, distributed, or transmitted in any form or by any means without the prior written permission of the author.

Unless otherwise indicated, all Scripture quotations are from the New King James Version®. Copyright © 1982 by Thomas Nelson. Used by permission. All rights reserved.

ISBN: 979-824-4304-43-5

Printed in the United States of America

First Edition

Dedication

To the members of Sun Garden

You have been my family in the faith, my fellow pilgrims on this narrow road. These sermons were not crafted in solitude but forged in the furnace of our life together. You have been patient with me as I have grown. You listened when my words stumbled. You encouraged when my spirit flagged. You forgave when I fell short of the calling. A congregation shapes its preacher as much as any preacher shapes his congregation, and whatever good has come from this pulpit, you have had a hand in it.

To my fellow elder, who shares the weight of shepherding these souls, thank you for standing with me when the decisions were difficult. The flock is safer because we watch together.

To the deacons, who serve without seeking recognition, who meet needs before they are spoken, who carry burdens so that others may walk lighter, you are the hands and feet of Christ among us.

To the teachers, who week after week open the Scriptures and attend to the spiritual needs of this body with faithfulness and care, you plant seeds that will bear fruit for generations. Eternity alone will reveal the harvest of your labors.

And to the women who quietly serve in faith and love, you who prepare meals for the grieving, who send cards to the forgotten, who pray when no one is watching, who teach the children and mentor the young wives, who hold this church together in a thousand ways that never make the announcements, God sees. He remembers. And one day He will say to you, "Well done."

This book belongs to all of you.

"I thank my God upon every remembrance of you, always in every prayer of mine making request for you all with joy, for your fellowship in the gospel from the first day until now."
Philippians 1:3-5

Table of Contents

Prologue: An Invitation to the Journey   1

Chapter One: Hearing the Word of God   7

Chapter Two: Believing the Word of God   21

Chapter Three: Repentance Based on the Word of God   37

Chapter Four: Confessing Jesus Christ   51

Chapter Five: The Necessity of Baptism   67

Chapter Six: Walking in Holiness   83

Conclusion: The Door Stands Open   103

Recommended Resources   111

Prologue

An Invitation to the Journey

Dear Reader,

If you have picked up this book, perhaps you are searching for something. Perhaps you sense that there is more to life than what you have experienced, more to faith than what you have been told, more to God than what you have yet discovered. Perhaps you stand at a crossroads, uncertain which path leads to life, and which leads to emptiness. Or perhaps you have walked with Christ for many years and simply desire to understand more deeply the foundations upon which your faith rests.

Whatever has brought you to these pages, I want you to know that you are welcome here. This book was not written from a place of spiritual superiority or theological arrogance. It was written by a fellow traveler, one who has walked the same road you are walking, one who has asked the same questions you are asking, one who has needed the same grace you need. I do not write as one who has arrived but as one who is still on the journey, still learning, still growing, still depending daily upon the mercy of God.

The subject of this book is nothing less than the most important question any human being can ask: **What must I do to be saved?** This question echoes through the pages of Scripture. It fell from the lips of the Philippian jailer as he trembled before Paul and Silas in that midnight hour. It was the cry of the multitude on Pentecost when Peter's sermon pierced their hearts. It is the question that every honest soul must eventually confront, for we all stand in need of salvation.

We need salvation because we are sinners. This is not a popular truth in our age, but it is truth, nonetheless. We have all fallen short of God's glory. We have all wandered from His ways. We have all chosen our own paths over His path, our own wisdom over His wisdom, our own desires over His commands. And the wages of this sin is death, eternal separation from the God who made us and loves us. This is the human condition, and no amount of positive thinking or self-improvement can change it.

But here is the good news that forms the heart of everything in these pages: God has provided a way of salvation. In His great love, He did not leave us to perish in our sins. He sent His only Son, Jesus Christ, to live the life we could not live and to die the death we deserved to die. On the cross, Jesus bore the punishment for our sins. In the tomb, He lay buried for three days. And on the third day, He rose victorious over death and the grave, declaring to all the world that salvation is possible, that forgiveness is available, that new life can begin.

This salvation is offered freely to all who will receive it. It cannot be earned by good works or religious rituals. It cannot be purchased with money or achieved through human effort. It is the gift of God, given by grace to undeserving sinners who will simply receive it on His terms.

And that is what this book is about: God's terms. How does a person receive this gift of salvation? What response does God require from those who would be saved? These are not questions we can answer according to our own preferences or traditions. They must be answered from Scripture, for the Bible alone is our authority in matters of faith and practice. What does the Lord say? That is the only question that ultimately matters.

The Journey Before Us

In the chapters that follow, we will trace the path of salvation as it is revealed in the Word of God. We will examine each step carefully, seeking to understand not merely what God commands but why He commands it. We will explore the rich meaning of the original Hebrew and Greek words, for often the depth of Scripture is hidden in the nuances of language that English translations cannot fully capture. And we will see how the Old Testament provides the foundation and background for understanding the New Testament's teaching on salvation.

Our journey begins with hearing. Faith comes by hearing, and hearing by the Word of God. Before we can believe, we must hear. Before we can respond, we must receive the message. The gospel must reach our ears and penetrate our hearts. We will discover what it truly means to hear God's Word, not merely with our physical ears but with understanding, attention, and a willingness to obey.

From hearing, we move to believing. But biblical faith is far more than intellectual agreement with certain facts. Even the demons believe and tremble. Saving faith involves the whole person: mind, heart, and will. It is trust that transforms, conviction that compels action, confidence in God that moves us to stake our eternal destiny upon His promises. We will examine the nature of this faith, its content, and its expression in the lives of those who truly believe.

Faith that is genuine will produce repentance. This is the turning point, the complete change of direction that marks the transition from death to life. Repentance is not merely feeling sorry for sin; it is a fundamental reorientation of the soul toward God. We will explore the difference between worldly sorrow that leads to death and godly sorrow that leads to life, and we will see what true repentance looks like in practice.

What the heart believes, the mouth must confess. Confession is faith made audible, belief given voice, the public declaration of our allegiance to Jesus Christ as Lord. We will consider why confession is essential, what we must confess, and how this confession connects us to the great company of believers who have made this same declaration throughout the centuries.

The journey then brings us to baptism, that sacred moment when we are buried with Christ in water and raised to walk in newness of life. Few subjects generate more controversy in the religious world, but we will let Scripture speak for itself. We will examine what baptism means, why it matters, and how it functions in God's plan of salvation. We will see that baptism is not a mere symbol of salvation already received but the divinely appointed means through which the penitent believer contacts the saving blood of Christ.

Finally, we will consider what it means to live as children of God. Salvation is not merely a moment of conversion but the beginning of a new life. We are called to walk in holiness, to present our bodies as living sacrifices, to be transformed by the renewing of our minds. The same grace that saves us also sanctifies us, and the journey of faith continues until we see our Lord face to face.

A Word About This Book

This book grew out of a series of sermons preached to a congregation I love dearly. These messages were delivered not as academic lectures but as pastoral exhortations to real people facing real decisions about their eternal destiny. I have tried to preserve that tone in these written pages. This is not primarily a theological treatise, though I trust it is theologically sound. It is an invitation, an appeal, a pleading with souls to respond to the gospel of Jesus Christ.

Throughout these chapters, you will notice frequent references to the original languages of Scripture. I include these not to impress but to illuminate. The Bible was not written in English, and sometimes the full meaning of a passage can only be grasped when we understand the words the Holy Spirit chose to employ. I have tried to make these references accessible to readers without any background in Hebrew or Greek, for the treasures of Scripture belong to all of God's people, not merely to scholars.

You will also notice that I draw heavily upon the Old Testament. Many treatments of salvation focus almost exclusively on the New Testament, but this approach impoverishes our understanding. The New Testament was written by Jews steeped in the Hebrew Scriptures, and they assumed their readers would understand the connections. When Peter spoke of baptism as the antitype of Noah's flood, his audience knew the story. When Paul described believers as priests offering sacrifices, his readers understood the imagery. We need the Old Testament to fully appreciate the New.

I have written with conviction, for I believe these truths with all my heart. But I have also tried to write with humility, for I am acutely aware of my own limitations and the ease with which any of us can misunderstand Scripture. I do not ask you to accept anything in these pages simply because I have said it. I ask you to examine the Scriptures for yourself, to test what you read against the Word of God, to be like the noble Bereans who searched the Scriptures daily to see whether the things they were being taught were so.

An Invitation

If you are not yet a Christian, I invite you to read these pages with an open heart. Consider the claims of Christ. Examine the evidence. Ask yourself whether the gospel message might be true. And if you become convinced that it is true, I urge you to respond. Do not harden your heart. Do not delay. Today is the day of salvation.

If you are already a believer, I invite you to deepen your understanding of the salvation you have received. There is always more to learn, always more to appreciate, always more reason to give thanks. Perhaps as you read, you will be reminded of the grace that saved you and find your heart renewed in gratitude and devotion.

If you are a teacher or preacher, I offer these materials as a resource for your own ministry. Nothing in these pages is original to me; I have simply tried to faithfully present what Scripture teaches. Use whatever is helpful, adapt it to your own context, and may God bless your efforts to proclaim His Word.

Whatever your situation, I pray that God will use these pages to accomplish His purposes in your life. May His Spirit illumine your understanding as you read. May His Word take root in your heart and bear fruit in your life. And may you come to know, in ever deeper ways, the salvation that is found in Jesus Christ alone.

The journey begins with a single step. Let us take that step together.

Your fellow servant in Christ,

James Majors
Elder, Sun Garden Church of Christ
jmajors@sungardencoc.org

Chapter One
Hearing the Word of God

"So, then faith comes by hearing, and hearing by the word of God."
(Romans 10:17)

Introduction

Beloved brothers and sisters in Christ, we come together today to examine a subject that lies at the very foundation of our salvation: hearing the Word of God. In an age of constant noise and endless distraction, the ability to truly hear has become increasingly rare. We are bombarded with information from every direction. Voices compete for our attention at every moment of the day. Yet amidst all this clamor, one voice stands supreme: the voice of God speaking through His Word.

Scripture places immense emphasis on hearing, for it is the gateway through which faith enters the human heart. The apostle Paul, writing to the church at Rome, declared this foundational truth: *"So then faith comes by hearing, and hearing by the word of God"* (Romans 10:17). This single verse establishes an unbreakable chain: God's Word produces hearing, and hearing produces faith. Without hearing, there can be no faith. Without faith, there can be no salvation. Therefore, we must give careful attention to what it means to truly hear the Word of God. This is not merely an academic exercise or a theological curiosity. Our eternal destiny depends upon how we hear and respond to God's message.

I. The Hebrew Concept: Shama

To understand the biblical concept of hearing, we must examine the original languages of Scripture. In the Hebrew Old

Testament, the primary word for "hear" is shama (שָׁמַע). This word appears over 1,100 times in the Old Testament and carries a meaning far richer than merely perceiving sound.

> *Hebrew: shama (שָׁמַע): to hear, to listen, to obey, to understand*

Shama encompasses the entire process of hearing: perceiving the sound, understanding the meaning, and responding with obedience. In Hebrew thought, one has not truly heard unless one has obeyed. This is why the same word is often translated as both "hear" and "obey" depending on the context. The connection between hearing and obeying was so strong in the Hebrew mind that they were virtually inseparable concepts. To say, "I heard" was to say, "I will obey." To claim to have heard while refusing to obey was a contradiction in terms.

Consider the famous Shema, the central confession of the Jewish faith:

> *"Hear, O Israel: The LORD our God, the LORD is one! You shall love the LORD your God with all your heart, with all your soul, and with all your strength. And these words which I command you today shall be in your heart. You shall teach them diligently to your children, and shall talk of them when you sit in your house, when you walk by the way, when you lie down, and when you rise up." (Deuteronomy 6:4-7)*

The command "Hear, O Israel" is not merely an invitation to listen. It is a call to attentive reception that results in wholehearted love and obedience. To hear is to respond. To hear is to obey. To hear is to let God's words penetrate the heart and transform the life. The faithful Israelite was to keep these words in the heart, teach them to children, and speak of them constantly. This was true hearing: a complete integration of God's Word into every aspect of life.

Moses repeatedly emphasized this connection between hearing and obedience throughout his farewell address to Israel: *"Now, O*

Israel, listen to the statutes and the judgments which I teach you to observe, that you may live, and go in and possess the land which the LORD God of your fathers is giving you" (Deuteronomy 4:1). The purpose of hearing was clear: to observe, to live, to possess the promises of God. Hearing without observing was not true hearing at all. Life itself depended upon proper hearing.

The blessings of God were contingent upon hearing and obeying His voice. Moses declared these blessings:

> *"Now it shall come to pass, if you diligently obey the voice of the LORD your God, to observe carefully all His commandments which I command you today, that the LORD your God will set you high above all nations of the earth. And all these blessings shall come upon you and overtake you, because you obey the voice of the LORD your God." (Deuteronomy 28:1-2)*

Notice the phrase "diligently obey the voice." In Hebrew, this is literally "hearing, you shall hear," an emphatic construction that stresses the intensity and completeness of the hearing required. Casual, half-hearted hearing would not suffice. God demanded diligent, wholehearted attention to His Word.

The consequences of failing to hear were equally serious: "*But it shall come to pass, if you do not obey the voice of the LORD your God, to observe carefully all His commandments and His statutes which I command you today, that all these curses will come upon you and overtake you*" (Deuteronomy 28:15). The same Hebrew construction appears: failure to "hear" the voice of the Lord brings curses rather than blessings. Hearing was never neutral in Scripture; it always led to either blessing or curse, life or death.

II. The Greek Concept: Akouō

The Greek New Testament continues this rich understanding of hearing through the word akouō (ἀκούω).

> *Greek: akouō (ἀκούω): to hear, to listen, to understand, to heed*

Like its Hebrew counterpart, akouō carries the sense of attentive listening that leads to understanding and response. From this word we derive our English word "acoustics," but the biblical meaning goes far beyond mere sound reception. In the New Testament, akouō often implies not just hearing but heeding, not just receiving sound but receiving truth into the heart.

A related Greek word is hupakouō (ὑπακούω), which combines "under" (hupo) with "hear" (akouō).

> *Greek: hupakouō (ὑπακούω): to listen under, to obey, to submit to what is heard*

This word literally means to hear under authority, to submit to what is heard. It is the source of our English word "obey" and demonstrates the inseparable connection between hearing and obedience in Greek thought as well.

Jesus frequently used akouō in His teaching, often with the emphatic phrase, "*He who has ears to hear, let him hear!*" (Matthew 11:15). This phrase appears repeatedly throughout the Gospels and Revelation. It indicates that while many may physically hear, not all truly hear in the biblical sense. True hearing requires spiritual receptivity, not merely functional eardrums. Jesus used this phrase to call attention to the deeper meaning of His words. He was saying, in effect, "What I am telling you has profound significance; make sure you truly understand and respond."

The seven letters to the churches in Revelation each conclude with this same admonition: "*He who has an ear, let him hear what the Spirit says to the churches*" (Revelation 2:7). The Spirit is speaking. The question is whether we have ears to hear.

III. The Necessity of Hearing for Salvation

The Scriptures are abundantly clear that hearing the Word of God is absolutely essential for salvation. No one can be saved without first hearing the gospel message. Paul explains this necessity in his letter to the Romans:

> *"How then shall they call on Him in whom they have not believed? And how shall they believe in Him of whom they have not heard? And how shall they hear without a preacher? And how shall they be sent unless they are sent? As it is written: 'How beautiful are the feet of those who preach the gospel of peace, Who bring glad tidings of good things!'" (Romans 10:14-15)*

Notice the logical progression Paul establishes. Salvation requires calling on the Lord. Calling requires believing. Believing requires hearing. Hearing requires preaching. Preaching requires sending. Each link in this chain is essential; remove any one and the process breaks down.

This is why the church has been commissioned to preach the gospel to every creature (Mark 16:15). The lost cannot be saved if they do not hear, and they cannot hear unless someone proclaims the message to them. This places tremendous responsibility upon us who have heard and believed. We must share the message so that others may hear. Beautiful are the feet of those who bring the good news, because without that proclamation, no one could be saved.

IV. Examples of Hearing in Acts

The book of Acts provides numerous examples of this pattern in action.

On the day of Pentecost, the crowd heard Peter's sermon: *"Now when they heard this, they were cut to the heart, and said to Peter and the rest of the apostles, 'Men and brethren, what shall we do?'"* (Acts 2:37). They heard, they were convicted, they responded. The hearing produced faith, and faith demanded action. The result was the baptism of about three thousand souls that very day (Acts 2:41). This was true hearing: hearing that penetrated the heart and produced transformation.

When Philip went down to Samaria, the people heard and responded: "*And the multitudes with one accord heeded the things spoken by Philip, hearing and seeing the miracles which he did*" (Acts 8:6). The word translated "heeded" is from the Greek prosechō (προσέχω), meaning to hold the mind toward, to give attention to, to be devoted to. The Samaritans did not merely hear; they gave careful, devoted attention to Philip's message. The result was belief and baptism (Acts 8:12).

When the Ethiopian eunuch encountered Philip on the desert road, he was reading from the prophet Isaiah but could not understand what he read. Philip asked him, "*Do you understand what you are reading?*" And he said, "*How can I, unless someone guides me?*" (Acts 8:30-31). The eunuch was reading but not understanding. He needed someone to explain the meaning. Philip "preached Jesus to him" (Acts 8:35), and the eunuch heard, believed, and was baptized. Hearing required not just the words but the understanding of their meaning.

When Cornelius gathered his household to hear Peter, the centurion declared: "*Now therefore, we are all present before God, to hear all the things commanded you by God*" (Acts 10:33). Cornelius understood that hearing what God commanded was essential. He gathered everyone together specifically for this purpose. They were present "before God" to hear "all the things" God had commanded. This is the proper attitude toward hearing God's Word: reverent, expectant, complete. The result was the conversion of the first Gentile household.

When Lydia encountered Paul at the riverside in Philippi, Luke records: "*The Lord opened her heart to heed the things spoken by Paul*" (Acts 16:14). Lydia heard, and the Lord opened her heart to heed. This reminds us that while we are responsible to hear, it is ultimately God who opens hearts to receive His truth. Human responsibility and divine initiative work together in the process of salvation.

When Paul and Silas were imprisoned in Philippi, the jailer asked what he must do to be saved. The apostles responded:

"Believe on the Lord Jesus Christ, and you will be saved, you and your household." Then they spoke the word of the Lord to him and to all who were in his house. And he took them the same hour of the night and washed their stripes. And immediately he and all his family were baptized (Acts 16:31-33). Notice carefully: before the jailer could believe, Paul and Silas "spoke the word of the Lord to him." He had to hear before he could believe. The instruction to "believe" was not complete without the proclamation of what to believe. The pattern is consistent throughout the New Testament: hearing precedes faith, and faith precedes obedience.

V. The Parable of the Sower: Different Kinds of Hearers

While hearing is essential, Scripture warns us that not all hearing is equal. There is a vast difference between hearing with the ear and hearing with the heart. Many people hear the same message, yet respond in vastly different ways. Jesus addressed this distinction in His parable of the sower:

> *"Therefore, hear the parable of the sower: When anyone hears the word of the kingdom, and does not understand it, then the wicked one comes and snatches away what was sown in his heart. This is he who received seed by the wayside. But he who received the seed on stony places, this is he who hears the word and immediately receives it with joy; yet he has no root in himself, but endures only for a while. For when tribulation or persecution arises because of the word, immediately he stumbles. Now he who received seed among the thorns is he who hears the word, and the cares of this world and the deceitfulness of riches choke the word, and he becomes unfruitful. But he who received seed on the good ground is he who hears the word and understands it, who indeed bears fruit and produces: some a hundredfold, some sixty, some thirty." (Matthew 13:18-23)*

In this parable, all four types of soil represent people who "hear the word." Yet only one type produces fruit.

The wayside hearer hears but does not understand, and the word is snatched away by the evil one. This person allows the word to lie on the surface of the heart without penetrating. Satan easily removes what was never truly received.

The stony ground hearer hears and receives with joy, but has no depth and falls away under pressure. This person experiences an emotional response but lacks the depth of commitment to endure difficulty. When tribulation or persecution comes because of the word, this hearer stumbles immediately.

The thorny ground hearer hears, but worldly cares and the pursuit of riches choke the word into unfruitfulness. This person allows competing concerns to crowd out the word. The word is not rejected outright but is slowly suffocated by other priorities.

Only the good ground hearer truly hears: receiving the word, understanding it, and bearing fruit. This person has a heart prepared to receive, a mind open to understand, and a will ready to obey. The result is fruitfulness: some thirtyfold, some sixty, some a hundred.

This parable teaches us that the condition of the heart determines the effectiveness of the hearing. The seed is the same; the sower is the same; only the soil differs. We must examine our own hearts: What kind of soil am I?

VI. The Danger of Hearing Without Heeding

The prophet Isaiah spoke of those who hear but do not truly hear: *"Seeing many things, but you do not observe; opening the ears, but he does not hear"* (Isaiah 42:20). Physical hearing without spiritual receptivity is no hearing at all. The ears were open, but no true hearing occurred. Eyes saw many things, but there was no observation, no perception, no understanding.

Jesus quoted Isaiah when explaining why He spoke in parables:

> *"And in them the prophecy of Isaiah is fulfilled, which says: 'Hearing you will hear and shall not understand, and seeing you will see and not perceive; for the hearts of this people have grown dull. Their ears are hard of hearing, and their eyes they have closed, lest they should see with their eyes and hear with their ears, lest they should understand with their hearts and turn, so that I should heal them.'" (Matthew 13:14-15)*

The problem was not auditory; it was spiritual. Their hearts had grown dull. Their ears were hard of hearing. Their eyes were deliberately closed. They refused to hear because they did not want to turn and be healed. This is the tragedy of willful spiritual deafness: the cure is available, but it is rejected. Jesus offered healing, but they would not hear.

VII. How to Hear Properly

James, the Lord's brother, provides essential instruction on how to hear properly:

> *"So then, my beloved brethren, let every man be swift to hear, slow to speak, slow to wrath; for the wrath of man does not produce the righteousness of God. Therefore lay aside all filthiness and overflow of wickedness, and receive with meekness the implanted word, which is able to save your souls. But be doers of the word, and not hearers only, deceiving yourselves. For if anyone is a hearer of the word and not a doer, he is like a man observing his natural face in a mirror; for he observes himself, goes away, and immediately forgets what kind of man he was. But he who looks into the perfect law of liberty and continues in it, and is not a forgetful hearer but a doer of the work, this one will be blessed in what he does." (James 1:19-25)*

James teaches us several crucial principles about proper hearing.

First, we must be swift to hear. Eagerness and readiness should characterize our approach to God's Word. We should come to

Scripture with anticipation, not reluctance. We should hunger for God's truth as a starving man hungers for food.

Second, we must be slow to speak. Too often we are more interested in expressing our own opinions than in receiving divine instruction. We want to talk when we should be listening. We want to argue when we should be learning. The wise person listens more than speaks.

Third, we must be slow to wrath. Anger hinders hearing. When we become defensive or hostile toward God's Word, we cannot receive it properly. The wrath of man does not produce the righteousness of God.

Fourth, we must lay aside all filthiness and wickedness. Sin in the life hinders the reception of the Word. A heart filled with wickedness has no room for truth. We must cleanse ourselves to receive the pure Word of God.

Fifth, we must receive the Word with meekness. A humble, teachable spirit is essential for proper hearing. Pride resists instruction; meekness welcomes it. The meek heart says, "Lord, teach me; I am ready to learn and obey."

Sixth, and most importantly, we must be doers of the Word, not hearers only. To hear without doing is to deceive oneself. It is like looking in a mirror and immediately forgetting what you saw. What good is seeing your reflection if you take no action based on what you see? True hearing always results in action. The one who looks into the perfect law of liberty and continues in it, being a doer and not a forgetful hearer, will be blessed.

VIII. Solemn Warnings About Hearing

The writer of Hebrews issues a solemn warning about the danger of hearing without heeding:

> "Therefore, we must give the more earnest heed to the things we have heard, lest we drift away. For if the word spoken through angels proved steadfast, and every transgression

and disobedience received a just reward, how shall we escape if we neglect so great a salvation, which at the first began to be spoken by the Lord, and was confirmed to us by those who heard Him." (Hebrews 2:1-3)

The danger is not merely failing to hear, but failing to heed what we have heard. Neglecting what we have heard leads to drifting away. The drift is gradual, almost imperceptible, but ultimately devastating. And if those who violated the law given through angels received just punishment, how much greater will be the punishment for those who neglect the salvation spoken by the Lord Himself? Greater revelation brings greater responsibility. We who have heard the gospel of Christ are more accountable than those who heard only the Law of Moses.

Later in the same epistle, the writer warns: "*See that you do not refuse Him who speaks. For if they did not escape who refused Him who spoke on earth, much more shall we not escape if we turn away from Him who speaks from heaven*" (Hebrews 12:25). God is speaking. The question is whether we will hear and heed, or refuse and face the consequences. Those who refused the voice at Sinai did not escape judgment. How much less shall we escape if we refuse the voice from heaven?

Jesus concluded His Sermon on the Mount with a powerful illustration of the two kinds of hearers:

"Therefore, whoever hears these sayings of Mine, and does them, I will liken him to a wise man who built his house on the rock: and the rain descended, the floods came, and the winds blew and beat on that house; and it did not fall, for it was founded on the rock. But everyone who hears these sayings of Mine, and does not do them, will be like a foolish man who built his house on the sand: and the rain descended, the floods came, and the winds blew and beat on that house; and it fell. And great was its fall." (Matthew 7:24-27)

Both men heard the same words. Both experienced the same storms. The difference was not in what they heard, but in what they did with what they heard. One heard and obeyed; his house stood firm against the storm. One heard and ignored; his house collapsed in ruin. The storms of life and judgment will reveal the quality of our hearing. When trials come, when temptations arise, when death approaches, our foundation will be tested. Only hearing that produces obedience will withstand the test.

IX. Examples of Proper Hearing

Scripture provides us with wonderful examples of those who heard properly and responded faithfully.

Samuel, as a young boy serving in the tabernacle, heard the voice of the Lord calling him. When he finally recognized it was God speaking, his response was exemplary: "*Speak, for Your servant hears*" (1 Samuel 3:10). This should be the posture of every child of God: "Speak, Lord, for Your servant hears." Not merely "I am listening," but "I am ready to obey." The servant posture indicates submission to whatever the Master commands. Samuel went on to become one of Israel's greatest prophets, faithfully delivering God's word to the people. His life of faithful service began with these simple words: "Speak, for Your servant hears."

Mary, the mother of Jesus, exemplified proper hearing when the angel announced God's plan for her life. Despite the impossibility of what was announced and the potential cost to her reputation, she responded: "*Behold the maidservant of the Lord! Let it be to me according to your word*" (Luke 1:38). She heard, she submitted, she obeyed. She did not argue or make excuses. She did not demand to understand how such a thing could be. She simply placed herself at God's disposal: "Let it be to me according to your word." This is true hearing: complete surrender to God's will as revealed in His Word.

The Bereans are commended for their manner of hearing: "*These were more fair-minded than those in Thessalonica, in that they received the word with all readiness, and searched the Scriptures daily to find out whether these things were so. Therefore many of them believed*" (Acts 17:11-12). They received the Word with readiness. They were open and eager to hear. They searched the Scriptures to verify what they heard. They did not blindly accept or blindly reject; they examined carefully. They did this daily, not just occasionally. The result was that many believed. This combination of receptivity and careful examination is the model for all who would hear God's Word properly.

X. The Danger of Familiarity

In our modern age, we have unprecedented access to the Word of God. Bibles are readily available in countless translations and formats. Sermons can be heard at any time through recordings, broadcasts, and internet streaming. Bible study resources abound in print and online. Never in human history has the Word of God been more accessible.

Yet with this abundance of access comes the danger of familiarity breeding contempt. We can become so accustomed to hearing that we no longer truly hear. The words pass through our ears without penetrating our hearts. We attend worship services, sit through sermons, participate in Bible classes, yet remain unchanged. This is the most dangerous form of deafness: the deafness that thinks it hears.

We may know the facts of Scripture without knowing the God of Scripture. We may be able to quote verses without being changed by them. We may have religion without relationship, knowledge without transformation. We must guard against becoming like those Jesus described: "*But why do you call Me 'Lord, Lord,' and not do the things which I say?*" (Luke 6:46). They called Him Lord. They heard His words. But they did not do what He said. This is not hearing in the biblical sense. To call Him Lord while refusing to obey Him is a contradiction. True hearing acknowledges His Lordship through obedience.

Brothers and sisters, we have examined the biblical doctrine of hearing the Word of God. We have seen from the Hebrew shama and the Greek akouō that true hearing involves far more than the physical perception of sound. True hearing is attentive: giving careful, focused attention to what God says. True hearing is understanding: grasping the meaning and significance of God's message. True hearing is obedient: responding to what is heard with faithful action.

Faith comes by hearing, and hearing by the Word of God. Without hearing, there can be no faith. Without faith, there can be no salvation.

The question for each of us today is this: How are you hearing? Are you like the wayside, where the word is snatched away before it can take root? Are you like the stony ground, receiving with joy but falling away when difficulty comes? Are you like the thorny ground, allowing worldly cares to choke the word into unfruitfulness? Or are you like the good ground, hearing, understanding, and bearing fruit?

If you have never truly heard and obeyed the gospel, today is your opportunity. The Word of God calls you to believe in Jesus Christ as the Son of God. It calls you to repent of your sins. It calls you to confess your faith before others. It calls you to be baptized for the remission of sins. Will you hear and obey? Will you respond as Samuel did: "Speak, Lord, for Your servant hears"? Will you respond as Mary did: "Let it be to me according to your word"?

If you are a Christian who has become dull of hearing, today is your call to renewal. Return to the Word with fresh eagerness. Receive it with meekness. Put away the sin that hinders your hearing. Be swift to hear, slow to speak, slow to wrath. Be a doer of the Word, not a hearer only. Give earnest heed to what you have heard, lest you drift away. Build your house upon the rock by hearing and doing.

Let us close with the words of our Lord: "He who has ears to hear, let him hear!" (Mark 4:9). May we all be those who truly hear. May we receive the Word with meekness and obedience. And may our lives bear the abundant fruit that demonstrates we have heard from God.

Chapter Two
Believing the Word of God

"But without faith it is impossible to please Him, for he who comes to God must believe that He is, and that He is a rewarder of those who diligently seek Him." (Hebrews 11:6)

Introduction

We continue our journey through God's plan of salvation. Last week, we examined the foundational step of hearing the Word of God. We learned that faith comes by hearing, and hearing by the Word of God. We discovered that the Hebrew word shama means not just to hear, but to hear with understanding and intention to obey. We explored how God has spoken to us through His Son in these last days.

But hearing alone does not save. The Word must be received with faith. The seed must fall on good soil. The message must be mixed with believing. Today, we examine the essential nature of believing, of genuine saving faith. This is not a secondary matter or optional addition to Christianity. Faith stands at the very heart of our relationship with God.

The writer of Hebrews declares with absolute clarity:

"But without faith it is impossible to please Him, for he who comes to God must believe that He is, and that He is a rewarder of those who diligently seek Him." (Hebrews 11:6)

Impossible. Not difficult, not challenging, but impossible. The Greek word is adunatos (ἀδύνατος), meaning without power, without ability, cannot be done. Without faith, we cannot please God. No amount of moral living, religious activity, or good intentions can substitute for faith. You may give all your goods to feed the poor. You may give your body to be burned. You may speak with the tongues of men and angels. But without faith, you cannot please God.

I. The Nature of Biblical Faith

But what exactly is this faith that Scripture demands? The Greek word for faith is pistis (πίστις), meaning conviction, confidence, trust, reliance, fidelity, faithfulness. It comes from the root peithō, meaning to persuade or be persuaded. Faith is being persuaded of God's truth and trusting in it completely.

Greek: pistis (πίστις): conviction, confidence, trust, reliance, fidelity, faithfulness

The verb form is pisteuō (πιστεύω), meaning to trust in, to rely upon, to commit to, to entrust oneself to. This word appears 248 times in the New Testament. It is the word used when Jesus said, "Believe in the Lord Jesus Christ and you will be saved."

Greek: pisteuō (πιστεύω): to trust in, to rely upon, to commit to, to entrust oneself to

Biblical faith is not mere intellectual acknowledgment. It is not simply agreeing with certain facts or doctrines. James warns us about the inadequacy of intellectual belief:

"You believe that there is one God. You do well. Even the demons believe-and tremble!" (James 2:19)

The demons have intellectual belief. They know God exists. They recognize Jesus as the Holy One of God. In Mark 1:24, a demon cried out: "*Let us alone! What have we to do with You, Jesus of Nazareth? Did You come to destroy us? I know who You are-the Holy One of God!*" Perfect theology from the mouth of a demon. Yet they remain condemned. Their belief produces trembling, not transformation. Their knowledge brings fear, not faith.

Saving faith transcends mental assent. It involves the whole person: mind, heart, and will. The mind must understand the truth. The heart must embrace the truth. The will must act upon the truth.

II. Abraham: The Father of Faith

Consider Abraham, whom Scripture calls the father of faith:

> *"And he believed in the LORD, and He accounted it to him for righteousness." (Genesis 15:6)*

This verse is quoted three times in the New Testament. Paul quotes it in Romans 4:3 and Galatians 3:6. James quotes it in James 2:23.

The Hebrew word here is 'aman (אמן), meaning to support, to confirm, to be faithful, to trust, to be established, to be firm. From this root comes our word "Amen," meaning "so be it," "truly," "let it be established." When we say "Amen," we declare our agreement and trust in what has been said.

> *Hebrew: 'aman (אמן): to support, to confirm, to be faithful, to trust, to be established, to be firm*

Abraham's faith was not passive acknowledgment but active trust. God promised him descendants as numerous as the stars. At that moment, Abraham was childless and advanced in years. His wife Sarah was barren and past childbearing age. By all human calculation, God's promise was impossible. Yet Abraham believed.

Paul describes Abraham's faith in Romans 4:

> *"And not being weak in faith, he did not consider his own body, already dead (since he was about a hundred years old), and the deadness of Sarah's womb. He did not waver at the promise of God through unbelief, but was strengthened in faith, giving glory to God, and being fully convinced that what He had promised He was also able to perform." (Romans 4:19-21)*

Abraham faced the facts but trusted the promise. He acknowledged reality but believed in God's greater power. His faith was not denial of circumstances but confidence in God's character. And his faith produced action. When God called him to leave Ur, he left, not knowing where he was going. When God promised a son, he waited patiently for twenty-five years. When God commanded him to offer Isaac, he rose early in the morning to obey.

Hebrews 11:17-19 tells us:

"By faith Abraham, when he was tested, offered up Isaac, and he who had received the promises offered up his only begotten son, of whom it was said, 'In Isaac your seed shall be called,' concluding that God was able to raise him up, even from the dead, from which he also received him in a figurative sense." (Hebrews 11:17-19)

Abraham believed God could raise the dead. This was fifteen hundred years before any recorded resurrection in Scripture. He had never seen anyone raised from the dead. Yet he believed God's power extended even over death. This is faith: trusting God's Word enough to act upon it.

III. The Content of Saving Faith

Now, what must we believe to be saved? Scripture is precise about the content of saving faith. We are not left to wonder or speculate. God has clearly revealed what we must believe.

First, we must believe that God exists. *"For he who comes to God must believe that He is..."* (Hebrews 11:6a). Not just any god, but the God revealed in Scripture. The God who declares Himself in Exodus 3:14: "I AM WHO I AM." The self-existent, eternal, unchanging God. The God of Abraham, Isaac, and Jacob. The God who created all things and sustains them by His power. The God who is holy, just, merciful, and love.

Second, we must believe that God rewards those who seek Him. *"...and that He is a rewarder of those who diligently seek Him"* (Hebrews 11:6b). This speaks to God's character and His promises. We must believe that God is good, that He keeps His Word, that He desires our salvation.

The word "diligently" is important. The Greek word is ekzēteō (ἐκζητέω), meaning to seek out, to search carefully, to investigate, to crave. God rewards those who earnestly pursue Him.

Greek: ekzēteō (ἐκζητέω): to seek out, to search carefully, to investigate, to crave

Jesus promised: "*Ask, and it will be given to you; seek, and you will find; knock, and it will be opened to you. For everyone who asks receives, and he who seeks finds, and to him who knocks it will be opened*" (Matthew 7:7-8).

Third, and most specifically, we must believe in Jesus Christ. Jesus Himself declared:

"For God so loved the world that He gave His only begotten Son, that whoever believes in Him should not perish but have everlasting life." (John 3:16)

This may be the most familiar verse in all of Scripture. Yet its familiarity must not diminish its profound truth. Notice: whoever believes in Him. Not just believes about Him but believes in Him. The preposition matters greatly. In Greek, it is eis, meaning "into." To believe into Christ suggests movement, commitment, union. We place our faith into Him, resting our entire weight upon Him.

IV. What We Must Believe About Jesus

But what specifically must we believe about Jesus? We must believe that He is the Christ, the Son of God. John writes at the conclusion of his Gospel:

"But these are written that you may believe that Jesus is the Christ, the Son of God, and that believing you may have life in His name." (John 20:31)

The entire Gospel of John was written to produce this specific faith. Every sign, every discourse, every encounter points to this truth. Jesus is the Christ, the Messiah, the Anointed One promised throughout the Old Testament. Jesus is the Son of God, divine in nature, one with the Father.

We must believe in His incarnation:

> "By this you know the Spirit of God: Every spirit that confesses that Jesus Christ has come in the flesh is of God, and every spirit that does not confess that Jesus Christ has come in the flesh is not of God." (1 John 4:2-3a)

The Word became flesh and dwelt among us. God took on human nature. The eternal entered time. The infinite became an infant. This is the mystery of the incarnation, and we must believe it.

We must believe in His sinless life:

> "For He made Him who knew no sin to be sin for us, that we might become the righteousness of God in Him." (2 Corinthians 5:21)

Jesus lived the life we should have lived. He faced every temptation yet never sinned. He fulfilled all righteousness. He kept the law perfectly in thought, word, and deed.

We must believe in His death for our sins:

> "For I delivered to you first of all that which I also received: that Christ died for our sins according to the Scriptures." (1 Corinthians 15:3)

His death was not an accident or tragedy. It was not merely an example of sacrificial love. He died in our place, bearing our sins, suffering our punishment. Isaiah prophesied: "*But He was wounded for our transgressions, He was bruised for our iniquities; the chastisement for our peace was upon Him, and by His stripes we are healed. All we like sheep have gone astray; we have turned, every one, to his own way; and the LORD has laid on Him the iniquity of us all*" (Isaiah 53:5-6).

We must believe in His resurrection:

> "If you confess with your mouth the Lord Jesus and believe in your heart that God has raised Him from the dead, you will be saved." (Romans 10:9)

The resurrection is not optional to Christian faith. It is not a later addition or mythological embellishment. It is the cornerstone of the gospel. Paul declares with devastating clarity:

> *"And if Christ is not risen, then our preaching is empty and your faith is also empty. Yes, and we are found false witnesses of God, because we have testified of God that He raised up Christ, whom He did not raise up-if in fact the dead do not rise. For if the dead do not rise, then Christ is not risen. And if Christ is not risen, your faith is futile; you are still in your sins!" (1 Corinthians 15:14-17)*

Without the resurrection, we have no gospel, no hope, no salvation. Christianity stands or falls on the empty tomb. But Christ is risen! The tomb is empty! Death is defeated! And we must believe it.

We must believe that Jesus is Lord:

> *"Therefore, let all the house of Israel know assuredly that God has made this Jesus, whom you crucified, both Lord and Christ." (Acts 2:36)*

To believe Jesus is Lord means to acknowledge His authority over our lives. He is not just Savior but also Master. He is not merely our helper but our ruler. He does not come to assist us in our plans but to direct our paths.

We must believe in His ascension and present ministry:

> *"Therefore, He is also able to save to the uttermost those who come to God through Him, since He always lives to make intercession for them." (Hebrews 7:25)*

Jesus did not leave us orphans. He ascended to the right hand of the Father. He serves as our High Priest, ever living to intercede for us. He prepared a place for us.

V. Faith and Works

Now let us consider the relationship between faith and works. This has been a point of confusion and controversy throughout church history. Wars have been fought, churches have divided, and souls have been confused over this issue. Yet Scripture is clear when properly understood.

Paul writes:

> *"For by grace you have been saved through faith, and that not of yourselves; it is the gift of God, not of works, lest anyone should boast." (Ephesians 2:8-9)*

We are saved by grace through faith, not by works. Salvation is a gift, not a wage. We receive it, we do not achieve it. No amount of good deeds can earn God's favor.

Yet James writes:

> *"What does it profit, my brethren, if someone says he has faith but does not have works? Can faith save him? If a brother or sister is naked and destitute of daily food, and one of you says to them, 'Depart in peace, be warmed and filled,' but you do not give them the things which are needed for the body, what does it profit? Thus also faith by itself, if it does not have works, is dead." (James 2:14-17)*

And again: "*You see then that a man is justified by works, and not by faith only*" (James 2:24).

Is this a contradiction? Does James contradict Paul? Absolutely not! Paul and James address different errors from different angles. Paul confronts legalism, the belief that we earn salvation through works of the Law. James confronts antinomianism, the belief that faith requires no response. Paul emphasizes the root of salvation: faith. James emphasizes the fruit of salvation: works. Paul answers the question: How is a person saved? James answers the question: How do we know a person is saved? Both are correct: we are saved by faith, but saving faith always produces works.

Consider the analogy of fire and heat. Fire produces heat, but heat does not produce fire. Yet wherever there is genuine fire, there will be heat. A fire without heat is not a fire at all. It may look like fire, it may be called fire, but if it produces no heat, it is not fire. So it is with faith and works. Faith produces works, but works do not produce faith. Yet wherever there is genuine faith, there will be works. Faith without works is not faith at all. It may claim to be faith, it may use the vocabulary of faith, but if it produces no transformation, it is not saving faith.

Even Paul, the apostle of justification by faith, immediately follows Ephesians 2:8-9 with verse 10:

> *"For we are His workmanship, created in Christ Jesus for good works, which God prepared beforehand that we should walk in them." (Ephesians 2:10)*

We are not saved by good works, but we are saved for good works. Works do not produce salvation, but salvation produces works.

Hebrews 11 demonstrates this principle repeatedly. This great chapter is often called the Hall of Faith. Yet it could equally be called the Hall of Faith in Action. By faith Abel offered a more excellent sacrifice. By faith Enoch walked with God. By faith Noah prepared an ark. By faith Abraham obeyed and went out. By faith Sarah received strength to conceive. By faith Moses refused to be called the son of Pharaoh's daughter. By faith the walls of Jericho fell down. By faith Rahab received the spies with peace. In each case, faith acted. Faith moved, faith responded, faith obeyed. Faith that does not act is not biblical faith.

VI. The Definition of Faith

This brings us to the nature of saving faith. Hebrews 11:1 provides a definition:

> *"Now faith is the substance of things hoped for, the evidence of things not seen." (Hebrews 11:1)*

The word "substance" translates the Greek hypostasis (ὑπόστασις), meaning that which stands under, foundation, confidence, assurance, reality. It is used in Hebrews 1:3 where Christ is called "the express image of His person." Faith provides the foundation for our hope. It gives substance to what we cannot yet see.

> *Greek: hypostasis (ὑπόστασις): that which stands under, foundation, confidence, assurance, reality*

The word "evidence" translates elenchos (ἔλεγχος), meaning proof, conviction, demonstration, evidence that convinces. It is the word used in 2 Timothy 3:16 for "reproof." Faith serves as proof of unseen realities. It convinces us of what our eyes cannot perceive.

> *Greek: elenchos (ἔλεγχος): proof, conviction, demonstration, evidence that convinces*

We cannot see God, but faith convinces us He exists. We cannot see heaven, but faith assures us it awaits. We cannot see the resurrection, but faith confirms Christ lives. We cannot see forgiveness, but faith knows our sins are gone.

This faith is not blind. It is not a leap in the dark. It is not believing without evidence. Faith rests upon evidence: the testimony of Scripture, the witness of creation, the transformation of lives, the testimony of the Spirit. But it transcends what eyes can see.

Paul writes: "*For we walk by faith, not by sight*" (2 Corinthians 5:7). And again: "*While we do not look at the things which are seen, but at the things which are not seen. For the things which are seen are temporary, but the things which are not seen are eternal*" (2 Corinthians 4:18). Faith sees the invisible. Faith grasps the eternal. Faith knows the unknowable.

VII. Faith in Action in Acts

Consider how faith operates in conversion. The book of Acts provides multiple examples of faith leading to salvation. In Acts

16, the Philippian jailer asks the most important question any person can ask:

> *"Sirs, what must I do to be saved?" So they said, "Believe on the Lord Jesus Christ, and you will be saved, you and your household." (Acts 16:30-31)*

The answer is clear: believe on the Lord Jesus Christ. But notice what follows. They spoke the Word of the Lord to him and all in his house. Faith requires content; they needed to know what to believe. He took them and washed their stripes. Faith produced immediate compassion and repentance. He and all his family were baptized immediately. Faith led to immediate obedience. He brought them into his house and set food before them. Faith expressed itself in hospitality and fellowship. He rejoiced, having believed in God with all his household. Faith produced joy.

His faith was not mere mental agreement. It transformed his actions, his relationships, his entire life. This pattern appears throughout Acts. On Pentecost, those who gladly received the word were baptized. The Samaritans believed Philip's preaching and were baptized. The Ethiopian eunuch believed and immediately requested baptism. Saul believed and arose and was baptized. Cornelius and his household believed and were baptized. Lydia's heart was opened, she attended to Paul's words, and she and her household were baptized. The Corinthians hearing, believed and were baptized. In every case, faith led to action. Just as Noah's faith led him to build an ark, their faith led them to be baptized.

VIII. Common Misconceptions About Faith

Now, let us address some common misconceptions about faith. These errors have confused and hindered many sincere seekers.

First misconception: faith is a feeling. Many wait for an emotional experience to confirm their faith. They expect a warm feeling, a tingling sensation, or an overwhelming emotion. They hear testimonies of others' dramatic experiences and wonder why they feel nothing. But faith is not feeling. Feelings come and go, but faith endures. Emotions fluctuate with circumstances, but faith stands on God's unchanging Word. Faith is taking God at His Word regardless of how we feel. Abraham did not feel the presence of descendants when God promised them. Noah did not feel raindrops when he built the ark. The Israelites did not feel dry ground when they stepped into the Jordan. The walls of Jericho looked as solid as ever when Israel marched around them. Faith acts on God's promises, not on feelings.

Second misconception: faith is inherited. Some assume they have faith because their parents were Christians. They grew up in the church and assume that makes them believers. They rest on their family's spiritual heritage rather than personal faith. But faith cannot be inherited. God has no grandchildren, only children. Each person must personally believe. John the Baptist warned the Pharisees: "*And do not think to say to yourselves, 'We have Abraham as our father.' For I say to you that God is able to raise up children to Abraham from these stones*" (Matthew 3:9). Physical descent from Abraham did not make them children of God. Neither does physical descent from Christian parents make us Christians. Jesus said: "*He who believes and is baptized will be saved; but he who does not believe will be condemned*" (Mark 16:16). Notice the individual nature: he who believes, he who does not believe. Each person must make their own decision.

Third misconception: faith is merely intellectual. Some equate faith with accepting certain facts about Jesus. They can recite the traditions, quote the verses, and argue the theology. They have perfect doctrine but imperfect devotion. Their minds are full of truth but their lives remain unchanged. This is not saving faith. Remember, even demons believe and tremble. They have orthodox theology but rebellious hearts. True faith transforms. Paul writes: "*Therefore, if anyone is in Christ, he is a new creation; old things have passed away; behold, all things have become new*" (2 Corinthians 5:17). A person may know all about Christ without knowing Christ. They may study Him without surrendering to Him. They may admire Him without adoring Him.

Fourth misconception: faith eliminates doubt. Some believe that any doubt disqualifies their faith. They struggle with questions and assume this means they lack faith. They hide their struggles, fearing others will judge them as unbelievers. But faith and doubt often coexist. Remember the father who brought his demon-possessed son to Jesus: "*Immediately the father of the child cried out and said with tears, 'Lord, I believe; help my unbelief!'*" (Mark 9:24). I believe; help my unbelief. Faith and doubt mingled in the same heart. Perfect honesty before the Lord. Jesus did not reject him but granted his request. Even the apostles struggled with doubt. When they saw the risen Christ, Matthew records: "*When they saw Him, they worshiped Him; but some doubted*" (Matthew 28:17). They worshiped, but some doubted. Even in the presence of the risen Lord, doubt lingered. Faith is not the absence of doubt but trusting God in spite of doubt.

Fifth misconception: faith is a one-time decision. Some believe that faith is merely the moment of initial belief. They made a decision years ago and consider that sufficient. But biblical faith is ongoing, continuous, persevering. The Greek present tense often used for believing indicates continuous action. We are to keep on believing, continue trusting, persist in faith. Paul writes: "*I have been crucified with Christ; it is no longer I who live, but Christ lives in me; and the life which I now live in the flesh I live by faith in the Son of God, who loved me and gave Himself for me*" (Galatians 2:20). Present tense: I live by faith. Not I lived by faith once, but I continually live by faith.

IX. How to Develop and Strengthen Faith

How then do we develop and strengthen faith?

First, through the Word of God. "*So then faith comes by hearing, and hearing by the word of God*" (Romans 10:17). The more we expose ourselves to God's Word, the stronger our faith grows. The Word reveals God's character, promises, and faithfulness. It shows us His power in history and His plan for the future. It testifies of Christ and builds our confidence in Him.

Second, through prayer. The disciples recognized their need for greater faith: "*And the apostles said to the Lord, 'Increase our faith'*" (Luke 17:5). We too can ask God to increase our faith. In prayer, we commune with God, experience His presence, and learn to trust Him.

Third, through obedience. Each act of obedience strengthens faith for the next step. Faith grows by exercise. When we trust God in small things and see His faithfulness, we learn to trust Him in greater things.

Fourth, through fellowship:

> *"And let us consider one another in order to stir up love and good works, not forsaking the assembling of ourselves together, as is the manner of some, but exhorting one another, and so much the more as you see the Day approaching." (Hebrews 10:24-25)*

The faith of others encourages our own faith. Their testimonies strengthen us. Their examples inspire us. Their prayers support us.

Fifth, through trials. James writes: "*My brethren, count it all joy when you fall into various trials, knowing that the testing of your faith produces patience*" (James 1:2-3). Trials test and strengthen faith. In difficulties, we learn to depend on God rather than ourselves. We discover His sufficiency in our weakness.

Faith steps out. Faith commits. Faith trusts. We must transfer our trust from ourselves to Christ. We must rely on His righteousness, not our own. We must rest our eternal destiny entirely upon Him. Saving faith commits everything to Jesus.

As we prepare for our invitation, consider the words of Jesus:

> *"Most assuredly, I say to you, he who believes in Me has everlasting life." (John 6:47)*

Has everlasting life. Not will have, but has. Present tense. Present possession. The moment we truly believe, and are buried in Christ, life begins. Not after death, but now. This is the power of faith. It connects us to Christ. It appropriates His sacrifice. It receives His righteousness. It secures His promises. It unites us with Him forever.

Brothers and sisters, without faith it is impossible to please God. But with faith, all things become possible. Jesus said to him, "*If you can believe, all things are possible to him who believes*" (Mark 9:23). Faith moves mountains of impossibility. Faith conquers kingdoms of darkness. Faith obtains promises of God. Faith stops the mouths of lions. Faith quenches the violence of fire. Faith escapes the edge of the sword. Faith turns weakness into strength. Faith receives the dead raised to life. But most importantly, faith saves the soul.

You have heard the Word of God. Now you must believe it. Will you take that step of faith today? Will you trust Jesus Christ with your eternal destiny? Will you move from mere hearing to genuine believing? Will you transfer your trust from yourself to the Savior? The choice is yours. But know this: faith is not optional. Without it, we cannot please God. Without it, we cannot be saved. Without it, we have no hope. But with faith, even faith as small as a mustard seed, we can move mountains.

Choose faith. Choose life. Choose Christ. And may your faith, though tested by fire, be found to praise, honor, and glory at the revelation of Jesus Christ.

Chapter Three
Repentance Based on the Word of God

"I tell you, no; but unless you repent you will all likewise perish." (Luke 13:3)

Introduction

We have been engaged in a series of lessons concerning God's plan of salvation. Thus far, we have examined the necessity of hearing the Word of God and the essential nature of faith. This morning, we turn our attention to what may be the most difficult step of all: repentance.

It is difficult because it requires something that runs contrary to our human nature. It requires us to acknowledge that we have been wrong. It demands that we confess we have been traveling in the wrong direction and that we must change our course. Human pride resists such admissions. We are inclined to justify ourselves. We are prone to explain away our failures or to compare ourselves with those we deem worse than ourselves. But God calls us to a different standard. He calls us to repent.

Let us begin with the words of our Lord in the Gospel of Luke, chapter 13. On this occasion, certain individuals came to Jesus with a report of a tragic event. Pilate had slain some Galileans while they were in the very act of offering sacrifices. It was a terrible atrocity. The implication behind their report seems to have been that these Galileans must have been exceptional sinners to have suffered such a fate.

Notice carefully the response of our Lord:

> *"And Jesus answered and said to them, 'Do you suppose that these Galileans were worse sinners than all other Galileans, because they suffered such things? I tell you, no; but unless you repent you will all likewise perish. Or those eighteen on whom the tower in Siloam fell and killed them, do you think that they were worse sinners than all other men who dwelt in Jerusalem? I tell you, no; but unless you repent you will all likewise perish.'" (Luke 13:2-5)*

Observe that Jesus stated this warning twice. "Unless you repent you will all likewise perish." Twice in three verses, the Lord issues this solemn declaration. When our Lord repeats a statement, we would do well to give it our most earnest attention. He does not say, "It would be beneficial if you repented." He does not suggest that repentance is merely one option among many. He declares, "Unless you repent, you will perish." The message could not be more clear. Repentance is not optional. It is a matter of spiritual life and death.

I. The Meaning of Repentance

Before we proceed further, let us establish clearly what repentance means according to the Scriptures. There is considerable confusion on this matter. Some suppose that repentance is merely feeling remorse for one's actions. They equate repentance with that uncomfortable sensation of guilt. But that is not repentance; that is merely remorse. Others believe repentance is saying, "I am sorry." But one may say "I am sorry" without any genuine intention to change. One may express regret while fully intending to continue in the same course of conduct. That is not repentance.

Let us examine the words the Holy Spirit has chosen to convey this concept. In the Old Testament, the primary Hebrew word for repentance is shuwb (שׁוּב).

> *Hebrew: shuwb (שׁוּב): to turn back, to return, to change direction*

This word literally means to turn around, to reverse one's direction. Consider a man walking down a road, proceeding steadily in one direction. Shuwb means that man stops, turns completely around, and begins walking in the opposite direction. It is not a minor adjustment. It is a complete about-face.

Hear how God employs this word through the prophet Ezekiel:

> *"Say to them: 'As I live,' says the Lord GOD, 'I have no pleasure in the death of the wicked, but that the wicked turn from his way and live. Turn, turn from your evil ways! For why should you die, O house of Israel?'" (Ezekiel 33:11)*

"Turn, turn from your evil ways!" Do you perceive the urgency in the voice of Almighty God? He is pleading with His people. "Why should you die?" God takes no pleasure in the destruction of the wicked. Yet He requires that we turn from our sinful ways.

There is another Hebrew word, nacham (נחם), which emphasizes the emotional dimension of repentance.

> *Hebrew: nacham (נחם): to be grieved, to feel sorrow, to change one's mind*

This is the grief, the godly sorrow that accompanies genuine repentance. The prophet Joel employs this concept when he writes:

> *"'Now, therefore,' says the LORD, 'Turn to Me with all your heart, with fasting, with weeping, and with mourning.' So rend your heart, and not your garments; return to the LORD your God, for He is gracious and merciful, slow to anger, and of great kindness; and He relents from doing harm." (Joel 2:12-13)*

"Rend your heart, and not your garments." In that ancient culture, when one experienced grief or mourning, it was customary to tear one's garments as an outward expression of inner anguish. Over time, however, this practice became mere ritual. People would tear their garments without any genuine grief in their hearts. And God says, "Do not give Me external displays. Rend your heart. Let it be genuine." God is not interested in religious performances. He desires genuine, heartfelt repentance.

In the New Testament, the primary Greek word for repentance is metanoeō (μετανοέω).

> *Greek: metanoeō (μετανοέω): to change one's mind, to think differently afterward*

This word is derived from two components: meta, meaning "after" or "change," and nous, meaning "mind." Thus, metanoeō literally means to change one's mind, to think differently than before. But it is not merely an intellectual change. It is a change that affects everything: one's thinking, attitudes, actions, and entire direction in life.

When we consider the Hebrew and Greek together, we arrive at this understanding: repentance is a change of mind that leads to a change of direction. It is not merely feeling badly about sin. It is not merely expressing regret. It is a complete transformation of how one thinks and how one lives.

II. Godly Sorrow Versus Worldly Sorrow

There is an important distinction we must understand. The Apostle Paul explains it in his second letter to the Corinthians, chapter 7. Paul had written the Corinthian church a letter of correction, and they were grieved by it. But notice what Paul says about their grief:

> *"Now I rejoice, not that you were made sorry, but that your sorrow led to repentance. For you were made sorry in a godly manner, that you might suffer loss from us in nothing. For godly sorrow produces repentance leading to salvation, not to be regretted; but the sorrow of the world produces death." (2 Corinthians 7:9-10)*

Here we find the distinction: godly sorrow versus worldly sorrow. Worldly sorrow produces death. Godly sorrow produces repentance leading to salvation. What is the difference between them?

Worldly sorrow is being sorry one was discovered in sin. It is sorrow over the consequences of one's actions. It is sorrow that one's reputation has been damaged or relationships have been strained. But godly sorrow is sorrow that one has offended the Almighty. It is grief that one's sin contributed to the suffering of Christ upon the cross. It is a sorrow that looks upon what one has done and says, "How could I have done this against my Lord?"

Consider the example of Judas Iscariot. After he betrayed our Lord, the Gospel of Matthew records:

> *"Then Judas, His betrayer, seeing that He had been condemned, was remorseful and brought back the thirty pieces of silver to the chief priests and elders, saying, 'I have sinned by betraying innocent blood.' And they said, 'What is that to us? You see to it!' Then he threw down the pieces of silver in the temple and departed, and went and hanged himself." (Matthew 27:3-5)*

Judas was remorseful. He even made confession: "I have sinned." He attempted to return the money. But he did not truly repent. His sorrow led to death, not to life. He possessed worldly sorrow, not godly sorrow.

Now contrast this with the Apostle Peter. Peter denied the Lord three times. And when the rooster crowed and Jesus turned and looked upon him, Peter went out and wept bitterly. Peter was devastated by what he had done. But his sorrow led to repentance. He returned to the Lord. He was restored. He proclaimed the first gospel sermon on the Day of Pentecost. He devoted the remainder of his life to serving Christ. That is godly sorrow producing repentance leading to salvation.

Let each of us examine ourselves: which kind of sorrow do we experience when we sin? Are we sorry because of the consequences, or are we sorry because we have grieved the heart of God?

III. The Necessity of Repentance

Let us now consider why repentance is absolutely necessary. It begins with this simple truth: all have sinned. Paul makes this unmistakably clear in Romans chapter 3:

> *"For all have sinned and fall short of the glory of God."* (Romans 3:23)

All. Not some. Not most. All. Every person in this assembly. Every person who has ever lived, with the sole exception of our Lord Jesus Christ. All have sinned. And if all have sinned, then all stand in need of repentance.

Consider what Paul declared to the philosophers on Mars Hill in Athens:

> *"Truly, these times of ignorance God overlooked, but now commands all men everywhere to repent, because He has appointed a day on which He will judge the world in righteousness by the Man whom He has ordained. He has given assurance of this to all by raising Him from the dead."* (Acts 17:30-31)

God commands all men everywhere to repent. This is a command, not a suggestion. And it applies to everyone, everywhere. For what reason? Because God is a God of judgment. God executed judgment upon apostate Israel, just as Jesus had warned. And the proof that God means what He says is the resurrection of Jesus Christ from the dead. The resurrection stands as God's assurance that He will do exactly as He has declared. Each of us shall stand before the Lord to give an account of our lives. Repentance remains the only way to be prepared to meet our God.

On the Day of Pentecost, Peter proclaimed the gospel of Christ: His life, His death, His resurrection. And when the multitude was convicted of their sin, they asked the most important question any person can ask:

> *"Now when they heard this, they were cut to the heart, and said to Peter and the rest of the apostles, 'Men and brethren, what shall we do?'" (Acts 2:37)*

"What shall we do?" And here is Peter's inspired response:

> *"Then Peter said to them, 'Repent, and let every one of you be baptized in the name of Jesus Christ for the remission of sins; and you shall receive the gift of the Holy Spirit. For the promise is to you and to your children, and to all who are afar off, as many as the Lord our God will call.'" (Acts 2:38-39)*

Repent. That is the first word of Peter's answer. Not "Try harder." Not "Become a better person." Not "Simply pray and all will be well." Repent. Turn around. Change your mind concerning sin. Change your direction. And then be baptized for the remission of sins. Repentance stands at the very doorway of the kingdom. One cannot enter without it.

Some may wonder: why does God require repentance? Can He not simply forgive us? Consider this: God's forgiveness is freely offered, but we must be willing to receive it upon His terms. And repentance is one of His terms. Consider the matter carefully. If one were to approach God and say, "Lord, forgive my sin, but I have no intention of changing; I wish to continue in my present course," would that be genuine? Would that be sincere? Certainly not. One is not truly sorry for sin if one desires to continue sinning. That is merely regret over consequences. Repentance demonstrates that our faith is genuine. It proves that we truly believe what God has declared concerning sin.

IV. The Fruits of Repentance

Let us examine what true repentance looks like in practice. John the Baptist was in the wilderness, preaching repentance. And certain Pharisees and Sadducees came to be baptized. One might expect John to be pleased by this development. The religious leaders coming to him? That would seem to be a significant occasion. But observe how John responds:

> *"But when he saw many of the Pharisees and Sadducees coming to his baptism, he said to them, 'Brood of vipers! Who warned you to flee from the wrath to come? Therefore bear fruits worthy of repentance, and do not think to say to yourselves, "We have Abraham as our father." For I say to you that God is able to raise up children to Abraham from these stones.'" (Matthew 3:7-9)*

"Brood of vipers!" That is hardly a warm greeting. John perceived their hypocrisy immediately. They desired the baptism without the repentance. They wanted the religious observance without the transformed life. And John declared, "Bear fruits worthy of repentance." In other words, "Demonstrate it. Prove it. Let me see the evidence of genuine change." True repentance produces fruit. Where there is no fruit, there is no repentance.

One of the most instructive examples of repentance in Scripture is that of Zacchaeus. You will recall the account. He was a chief tax collector, which in that day meant he was considered both a traitor and a thief. He served the Roman oppressors and enriched himself by defrauding his own countrymen. But when Jesus came to his house, something remarkable occurred:

> *"Then Zacchaeus stood and said to the Lord, 'Look, Lord, I give half of my goods to the poor; and if I have taken anything from anyone by false accusation, I restore fourfold.' And Jesus said to him, 'Today salvation has come to this house, because he also is a son of Abraham; for the Son of Man has come to seek and to save that which was lost.'" (Luke 19:8-10)*

Observe what Zacchaeus did. He did not merely offer a casual apology. He gave half of his possessions to the poor. And to anyone he had defrauded, he restored fourfold. That is repentance with substance. That is not merely expressing regret; that is making restitution. And what did our Lord say? "Today salvation has come to this house." The repentance of Zacchaeus was genuine, and Jesus acknowledged it as such.

The Apostle Paul described his own ministry in similar terms. When he stood before King Agrippa, he declared:

> *"Therefore, King Agrippa, I was not disobedient to the heavenly vision, but declared first to those in Damascus and in Jerusalem, and throughout all the region of Judea, and then to the Gentiles, that they should repent, turn to God, and do works befitting repentance." (Acts 26:19-20)*

Repent, turn to God, and do works befitting repentance. That is the complete picture. One cannot have genuine repentance without the works that give evidence of it.

V. Repentance for Christians

There is an important truth we must not overlook. Repentance is not solely for those who have never obeyed the gospel. It is not something one does once at conversion and never considers again. Christians also need to repent.

Consider the letters to the seven churches in the book of Revelation. These are letters addressed to churches, to those who are already Christians. And repeatedly, the Lord calls them to repent.

To the church at Ephesus:

> *"Remember therefore from where you have fallen; repent and do the first works, or else I will come to you quickly and remove your lampstand from its place-unless you repent." (Revelation 2:5)*

They had abandoned their first love, and the Lord demanded, "Repent, or I will remove your lampstand."

To the church at Pergamos:

> *"Repent, or else I will come to you quickly and will fight against them with the sword of My mouth." (Revelation 2:16)*

To the church at Sardis:

> *"Remember therefore how you have received and heard; hold fast and repent. Therefore if you will not watch, I will come upon you as a thief, and you will not know what hour I will come upon you." (Revelation 3:3)*

To the church at Laodicea:

> *"As many as I love, I rebuke and chasten. Therefore be zealous and repent." (Revelation 3:19)*

"As many as I love, I rebuke and chasten." The Lord loves these congregations, and it is precisely because of His love that He calls them to repent. He will not allow them to drift toward destruction without warning. And if those churches stood in need of repentance, ought we not to examine ourselves as well?

The Apostle John writes to Christians:

> *"If we say that we have no sin, we deceive ourselves, and the truth is not in us. If we confess our sins, He is faithful and just to forgive us our sins and to cleanse us from all unrighteousness. If we say that we have not sinned, we make Him a liar, and His word is not in us." (1 John 1:8-10)*

If we claim to have no sin, we deceive ourselves. But if we confess, He is faithful and just to forgive. That confession, that acknowledgment of sin, is part of the ongoing repentance that characterizes the Christian life. We do not come to Christ and then cease to struggle with sin. We continue to turn from sin. We continue to confess. We continue to grow in holiness.

VI. The Blessings of Repentance

Let us now consider what happens when we repent. For this is the good news of the gospel. Peter proclaimed in Acts chapter 3:

> *"Repent therefore and be converted, that your sins may be blotted out, so that times of refreshing may come from the presence of the Lord." (Acts 3:19)*

Your sins blotted out. Erased. Removed entirely. And times of refreshing from the presence of the Lord. That is what repentance brings. Not merely relief from guilt, but genuine spiritual renewal.

And our Lord declared something remarkable concerning repentance:

> "I say to you that likewise there will be more joy in heaven over one sinner who repents than over ninety-nine just persons who need no repentance." (Luke 15:7)

More joy in heaven. When a sinner repents, heaven itself rejoices. The angels celebrate. God Himself delights in the return of the wayward soul. That is the heart of our Father. He is not waiting to condemn. He is waiting to welcome the penitent home.

But one must come to Him. One must turn. God will not compel anyone. He is patient, but that patience will not continue indefinitely. Peter writes:

> "The Lord is not slack concerning His promise, as some count slackness, but is longsuffering toward us, not willing that any should perish but that all should come to repentance." (2 Peter 3:9)

The patience of God is providing opportunity for repentance. But let none mistake His patience for permission to continue in sin. Let none suppose that because judgment has not yet come, it never will. He is granting time. Let us use it wisely.

VII. The Parable of the Prodigal Son

Permit me to illustrate the nature of repentance with one more passage from Scripture. It is perhaps the most beautiful picture of repentance in all the Bible. I speak of the parable of the prodigal son in Luke chapter 15.

You know the account well. A young man approached his father and demanded his inheritance before his father had even died. In that culture, such a request was tantamount to saying, "Father, I wish you were dead." It was an act of profound disrespect and cruelty. Yet the father granted his request. And the son took his inheritance, traveled to a distant country, and squandered everything in reckless living. Then a severe famine struck that land, and the son found himself in desperate circumstances. He took a job feeding swine and longed to fill his stomach with the pods the pigs were eating. That was the lowest point imaginable for a Jewish young man.

And then the Scripture records something profound:

> "But when he came to himself, he said, 'How many of my father's hired servants have bread enough and to spare, and I perish with hunger! I will arise and go to my father, and will say to him, "Father, I have sinned against heaven and before you, and I am no longer worthy to be called your son. Make me like one of your hired servants."'" (Luke 15:17-19)

"When he came to himself." That is the beginning of repentance. He awakened to the reality of his condition. He saw his situation as it truly was. And he made a decision: "I will arise and go to my father." That is the turning. That is shuwb in action. He did not merely feel sorry while remaining in the pigpen. He arose. He changed direction. He returned home.

And observe his confession: "Father, I have sinned against heaven and before you." He offered no excuses. He did not blame the famine or those who had taken advantage of him. He took full responsibility for his sin. "I have sinned."

Now observe how the father responded:

> "And he arose and came to his father. But when he was still a great way off, his father saw him and had compassion, and ran and fell on his neck and kissed him." (Luke 15:20)

"When he was still a great way off." The father had been watching. The father had been waiting. And when he saw his son approaching, he did not stand with arms folded, waiting for an apology. He ran. In that culture, it was considered undignified for an elderly man to run. But this father cared nothing for his own dignity. He cared only for his son. He ran and fell upon his neck and kissed him.

That is the heart of God toward the penitent sinner. He is not waiting to condemn. He is not keeping a record of every failure. He is watching the road, waiting for you to return. And when you do, He runs to meet you.

The father threw a celebration for his son. He placed a robe upon him and a ring on his finger and sandals on his feet. He declared, "This my son was dead and is alive again; he was lost and is found." That is what occurs when one repents. One who was dead in sin comes alive. One who was lost is found. And heaven celebrates.

Perhaps you are here this morning and you have never truly repented. You may have experienced regret over certain things. You may have said you were sorry. But you have never experienced that deep, godly sorrow that produces a genuine change of direction. Today is your day of opportunity. God is calling you to turn. Turn from sin. Turn to Him. Believe in Jesus Christ as the Son of God. Confess your faith. Be baptized for the remission of sins. And begin a new life, walking in a new direction.

Perhaps you are a Christian who has been drifting. Sin has gradually crept back into your life. You have abandoned your first love. You have become spiritually lukewarm. The Lord says to you what He said to those churches: "Repent." Return to Him. Confess your sin. Request the prayers of your brothers and sisters. Return to the path of faithfulness. God is faithful and just to forgive. He is not finished with you.

Remember the words of Joel: "Return to the LORD your God, for He is gracious and merciful, slow to anger, and of great kindness." That is our God. Gracious. Merciful. Patient. Kind. He awaits you with open arms. But you must turn. Will you?

Chapter Four
Confessing Jesus Christ

"If you confess with your mouth the Lord Jesus and believe in your heart that God has raised Him from the dead, you will be saved." (Romans 10:9)

Introduction

This morning, we continue our journey through God's plan of salvation. We have been building upon a foundation laid in previous lessons. In our first lesson, we discovered that faith comes by hearing, and hearing by the Word of God. We learned that the Hebrew word shama (שׁמע) means to hear with understanding and intention to obey. It is not passive reception but active engagement with the Word.

We explored the nature of saving faith. We discovered that the Greek word pistis (πίστις) means conviction, confidence, and trust that transforms the whole person. We learned that biblical faith is not mere intellectual acknowledgment but complete commitment to Christ. The demons believe and tremble, but their belief does not save them. Saving faith moves from the head to the heart and produces a changed life.

From faith, we turned to repentance, that complete change of mind and direction that marks the transition from the old life to the new. We learned that the Hebrew word shuwb means to turn back, to reverse course entirely, and that the Greek metanoeō speaks of a transformation in thinking that reshapes everything. We saw the difference between worldly sorrow, which is merely regret over consequences, and godly sorrow, which grieves over having offended the Holy One. We watched the prodigal son come to himself in the pigpen and make the decision that changed everything: "I will arise and go to my father." Repentance is not just feeling bad about sin. It is turning away from sin and turning toward God.

Today, we examine the fourth essential step: confession of Jesus Christ as Lord. This is not an optional addition to faith but its necessary expression. What the heart truly believes, the mouth must confess. Confession is faith made audible. It is belief given voice. It is the outward declaration of an inward reality.

Jesus Himself declared the eternal significance of our confession:

> *"Therefore, whoever confesses Me before men, him I will also confess before My Father who is in heaven. But whoever denies Me before men, him I will also deny before My Father who is in heaven." (Matthew 10:32-33)*

These words should arrest our attention immediately. Our eternal destiny hinges upon whether we confess or deny Jesus Christ. There is no middle ground, no neutral position. We either confess Him or deny Him. Silence in the face of opportunity is itself a form of denial. The stakes could not be higher. What we say about Jesus before men determines what Jesus will say about us before the Father.

I. The Biblical Meaning of Confession

Before we can appreciate the necessity of confession, we must understand what biblical confession truly means. The English word "confession" often carries negative connotations in modern usage. We think of confessing to a crime or admitting wrongdoing. But the biblical concept is far richer and more profound than mere admission of guilt.

The Greek word for confess is homologeō (ὁμολογέω). This word literally means "to say the same thing" or "to agree with." It is a compound word combining homos (ὁμός) meaning "same" and logos (λόγος) meaning "word" or "statement." To confess is to align our words with God's truth about Jesus Christ.

> *Greek: homologeō (ὁμολογέω): to say the same thing, to agree with, to confess*

When we confess Jesus as Lord, we are saying the same thing about Him that God says. We are agreeing with the Father's declaration at Jesus' baptism: *"This is My beloved Son, in whom I am well pleased"* (Matthew 3:17). We are affirming what God has revealed about His Son. Confession, then, is not merely our own opinion about Jesus. It is our public agreement with divine truth. It is speaking God's Word about God's Son.

The noun form of this word is homologia (ὁμολογία). This word appears in key passages about Christian profession. The writer of Hebrews exhorts us:

> *"Seeing then that we have a great High Priest who has passed through the heavens, Jesus the Son of God, let us hold fast our confession." (Hebrews 4:14)*

And again:

> *"Let us hold fast the confession of our hope without wavering, for He who promised is faithful." (Hebrews 10:23)*

Notice that our confession is something to be held fast. The Greek word for "hold fast" is katechō (κατέχω) which means to grip firmly, to retain securely, to keep possession of. Our confession is not a one-time utterance but a lifelong commitment. We grip it tightly and never let it go.

> *Greek: katechō (κατέχω): to grip firmly, to retain securely, to keep possession of*

II. The Direction of the Hand

In the Hebrew Scriptures, sin and salvation turn on a single image: the hand. Numbers 15 describes a sin for which there was no sacrifice. The text calls it sinning "with a high hand," beyad ramah. Picture it. A raised fist. A clenched hand lifted toward heaven. This is defiance, knowing what God commands and saying, "I don't care." For that sin, there was no lamb. No bull. No goat. The offender was cut off. The high hand closed the door to mercy.

But there is another hand in Scripture. When the Hebrew expressed confession, he used the word yadah (יָדָה). The Hebrew word means to throw or cast the hand, often in praise and acknowledgment.

> *Hebrew: yadah (יָדָה): to throw or cast the hand, to praise, to confess, to acknowledge*

Do you see the contrast? The sinner with a high hand raises his fist against God. The one who confesses casts his hand toward God. Same limb. Opposite direction. And the direction makes all the difference.

On the Day of Atonement, the high priest laid hands on the scapegoat. He would confess, yadah, all Israel's iniquities over that animal. Then the goat was sent into the wilderness, carrying those sins away forever. Confession is not just speaking words. Confession is transfer. You cannot hold onto your sin and confess it at the same time. The hand that clings is not the hand that casts.

What is the posture of your hand before God today? The high hand is always clenched, holding tightly to autonomy and self-will. But confession requires an open palm. You cannot throw something while your fist is closed. God says: Open your hand. Cast it toward Me. Let it go.

Another Hebrew word, nagad (נָגַד) means to declare openly, to announce, to make known. The prophets used this word when declaring God's truth to the nations. Biblical confession, therefore, is not a private whisper but a public declaration.

> *Hebrew: nagad (נָגַד): to declare openly, to announce, to make known*

When Israel praised God, they were publicly acknowledging His lordship and their allegiance to Him. It is not a timid suggestion but a bold announcement. It is not merely holding an opinion but declaring a truth. When we confess Jesus Christ, we are publicly declaring our allegiance to Him. We are openly announcing that we belong to Him. We are making known to the world where our loyalty lies. This understanding transforms how we view confession. It is not merely words spoken at baptism and then forgotten. It is a lifestyle of public identification with Jesus Christ.

III. The Necessity of Confession for Salvation

Having understood what confession means, we must now address its absolute necessity for salvation. Paul makes this necessity explicit in Romans 10:

> *"That if you confess with your mouth the Lord Jesus and believe in your heart that God has raised Him from the dead, you will be saved. For with the heart one believes unto righteousness, and with the mouth confession is made unto salvation." (Romans 10:9-10)*

Observe the structure of this passage carefully. Paul presents two inseparable requirements: belief and confession. With the heart one believes unto righteousness. With the mouth confession is made unto salvation. These are not alternatives but companions. They are not options but necessities. They are two sides of the same coin of saving faith.

Some have tried to separate these two, arguing that heart belief is what truly saves. They treat mouth confession as a mere expression of something already complete. But notice Paul's precise language. He does not say, "With the heart one believes unto salvation and with the mouth confession is made as an expression of that salvation." He says confession is made "unto salvation." The Greek preposition is eis (εἰς) meaning "into" or "unto." Confession moves us toward salvation. It is part of the saving process, not merely its aftermath.

Consider why this must be so. Faith that remains silent is faith that remains hidden. And hidden faith benefits no one, not even the one who claims to possess it. Jesus addressed this directly:

> *"For out of the abundance of the heart the mouth speaks."* (Matthew 12:34)

What fills the heart will eventually overflow through the mouth. If Christ truly dwells in the heart, confession of Christ will flow from the lips. If the lips remain silent about Christ, we must question whether Christ truly reigns in the heart.

The Apostle Paul understood this connection intimately. Writing to the Corinthians, he declared:

> *"And since we have the same spirit of faith, according to what is written, 'I believed and therefore I spoke,' we also believe and therefore speak."* (2 Corinthians 4:13)

Paul quotes from Psalm 116:10. He establishes a principle: true belief compels speech. Faith cannot remain silent. Genuine conviction demands expression. Those who truly believe will inevitably confess. This is not legalism but logic. This is not works-righteousness but the natural fruit of genuine faith. The heart that truly loves Jesus cannot keep that love secret. The soul that truly trusts Christ cannot remain silent about that trust.

IV. What Must We Confess?

If confession is essential, what exactly must we confess? Scripture gives us clear guidance on the content of our confession.

First, we must confess that Jesus is Lord. Romans 10:9 specifies that we confess "the Lord Jesus." The Greek word is kurios (κύριος). This is a word of supreme significance. In the Greek translation of the Old Testament, the Septuagint, kurios translates the divine name YHWH. When we confess Jesus as Lord, we are affirming His deity. We are declaring that Jesus shares the very nature of God. We are acknowledging His absolute sovereignty over all creation and over our individual lives.

Greek: kurios (κύριος): Lord, Master, the divine name; used for YHWH in the Septuagint

In the Roman Empire, citizens were required to confess "Caesar is Lord." This was not merely a political statement but a religious one. Caesar claimed divine honors. Early Christians faced a stark choice: confess Caesar as lord or confess Jesus as Lord. They could not do both. Many chose death rather than deny their Lord. When we confess Jesus as Lord, we are making the same exclusive claim. We are declaring that no other authority is ultimate in our lives. Not Caesar, not culture, not self, not sin. Jesus alone is Lord.

But lordship implies more than deity. It implies ownership and authority. To confess Jesus as Lord is to acknowledge that He owns us. We are not our own; we were bought with a price. To confess Jesus as Lord is to submit to His authority. His commands are not suggestions; His will is not optional.

Second, we must confess that Jesus is the Christ. The Greek word is Christos (Χριστός) which translates the Hebrew Mashiach (מָשִׁיחַ) meaning "the Anointed One." To confess Jesus as Christ is to affirm that He is the long-awaited Messiah of Israel. He is the fulfillment of every Old Testament prophecy. He is the seed of the woman who crushes the serpent's head. He is the seed of Abraham through whom all nations are blessed. He is the prophet like Moses whom all must hear. He is the priest after the order of Melchizedek. He is the king from the line of David whose throne is forever. He is the suffering servant of Isaiah 53. He is the Son of Man from Daniel's vision to whom all dominion is given. Every promise, every type, every shadow finds its fulfillment in Him.

Greek: Christos (Χριστός) / Hebrew: Mashiach (מָשִׁיחַ): the Anointed One, the Messiah

Third, we must confess that Jesus is the Son of God. When Martha confessed her faith, she declared:

> "Yes, Lord, I believe that You are the Christ, the Son of God, who is to come into the world." (John 11:27)

The sonship of Jesus is not adoptive but eternal. He is the eternally begotten Son, of one substance with the Father. He is not a created being elevated to divine status. He is God the Son, the second person of the Trinity. In Him, the fullness of deity dwells in bodily form. This confession of Jesus as Son of God is foundational to Christian faith. John writes:

> "Whoever confesses that Jesus is the Son of God, God abides in him, and he in God." (1 John 4:15)

This confession brings divine indwelling. God takes up residence in those who confess His Son. Such a promise should make us eager to confess, not reluctant.

Fourth, we must confess the resurrection. Romans 10:9 specifically mentions believing that God raised Jesus from the dead. The resurrection is not a peripheral doctrine but the cornerstone of Christianity. Paul declared to the Corinthians:

> "And if Christ is not risen, then our preaching is empty and your faith is also empty... And if Christ is not risen, your faith is futile; you are still in your sins!" (1 Corinthians 15:14, 17)

Without the resurrection, Christianity collapses. The resurrection validates every claim Jesus made. It demonstrates that the Father accepted the Son's sacrifice. It proves that death itself has been conquered. It guarantees our own future resurrection. When we confess Christ, we confess the risen Christ. Not a dead teacher but a living Lord. Not a martyred prophet but a reigning King. Not a memory but a present reality. He is alive, and we must confess Him as such.

V. Biblical Examples of Confession

Scripture provides numerous examples of confession that illuminate our understanding. These examples show us what confession looks like in practice.

Consider the Ethiopian eunuch in Acts 8. This man of great authority had traveled hundreds of miles to worship in Jerusalem. On his return journey, he was reading Isaiah but could not understand it. Philip was sent by the Spirit to explain the gospel. Beginning with Isaiah 53, Philip preached Jesus to the Ethiopian. When they came to water, the Ethiopian asked:

> "See, here is water. What hinders me from being baptized?" (Acts 8:36)

Philip's response is instructive:

> "If you believe with all your heart, you may." And he answered and said, "I believe that Jesus Christ is the Son of God." (Acts 8:37)

Notice several important elements in this confession. First, the confession preceded baptism. Before entering the water, the Ethiopian declared his faith. Second, the confession was specific. He did not merely say "I believe." He stated the content of his belief: "Jesus Christ is the Son of God." Third, the confession was personal. He said, "I believe," taking ownership of this faith. Fourth, the confession was wholehearted. Philip required belief "with all your heart." This was not casual assent but total commitment.

This Ethiopian's confession became the pattern for believers throughout the centuries. Before baptism, individuals confess their faith in Jesus Christ as the Son of God.

Consider Peter's confession at Caesarea Philippi. Jesus asked His disciples: *"Who do men say that I, the Son of Man, am?"* (Matthew 16:13). The disciples reported various opinions: John the Baptist, Elijah, Jeremiah, or one of the prophets. Then Jesus made the question personal: *"But who do you say that I am?"* (Matthew 16:15). Peter responded with the definitive confession:

> *"You are the Christ, the Son of the living God."* (Matthew 16:16)

Jesus' response reveals the significance of this confession:

> "Blessed are you, Simon Bar-Jonah, for flesh and blood has not revealed this to you, but My Father who is in heaven. And I also say to you that you are Peter, and on this rock I will build My church, and the gates of Hades shall not prevail against it." (Matthew 16:17-18)

Peter's confession was not derived from human reasoning but from divine revelation. The Father revealed the identity of the Son, and Peter confessed what was revealed. Upon this confession, this rock-solid declaration of who Jesus is, the church would be built. Every Christian stands in the line of those who have made this same confession.

Consider also the confession of Thomas. Thomas had doubted the resurrection. He demanded physical proof. When Jesus appeared and invited Thomas to touch His wounds, Thomas fell at His feet with the confession:

> "My Lord and my God!" (John 20:28)

This is perhaps the highest Christological confession in all of Scripture. Thomas acknowledged Jesus not only as Lord but explicitly as God. Notice that Jesus did not correct Thomas. He did not say, "No, I am not God." Instead, He accepted the confession as appropriate and true.

Consider Martha's confession before the raising of Lazarus. Jesus had told her that He was "the resurrection and the life." He asked if she believed this. Her response demonstrates mature faith:

> "Yes, Lord, I believe that You are the Christ, the Son of God, who is to come into the world." (John 11:27)

Martha confessed Jesus as Christ, Son of God, and the Coming One. Her confession encompassed His messianic identity, His divine nature, and His prophetic fulfillment. This confession came in the midst of grief, as her brother lay dead in the tomb. Yet her faith held firm, and her confession remained strong.

Each of these examples demonstrates that confession is concrete, specific, and deeply personal. It is not vague spirituality but clear declaration of who Jesus is.

VI. Why Public Confession Is Essential

Why does God require public confession? Why is private belief not sufficient? Several reasons emerge from Scripture.

First, public confession honors Christ. Secret faith treats Jesus as something to be ashamed of. It suggests that association with Him is embarrassing or dangerous. But Jesus deserves to be publicly honored, not privately hidden. He is the King of kings. He is the Lord of lords. He is the Name above every name. Such a King deserves public acclaim, not whispered acknowledgment.

Second, public confession benefits the confessor. There is something that happens in the human soul when we speak our faith aloud. It solidifies our commitment. It makes real what might otherwise remain abstract. When we publicly declare our allegiance to Christ, we cross a line. We move from private consideration to public commitment. We burn bridges behind us. This is psychologically and spiritually significant. Public confession strengthens private faith.

Third, public confession benefits others. When we confess Christ, others hear. Our confession may be the seed that leads to their salvation. Our courage may inspire their courage. Our faith may strengthen their faith. No one is saved by another's confession. But many are influenced toward salvation by hearing others confess.

Fourth, public confession distinguishes the church. The church is the community of confessors. It is composed of those who have publicly declared their faith. This public declaration creates visible boundaries. It distinguishes believers from unbelievers. It identifies those who belong to Christ. Without public confession, there would be no visible church. There would be only invisible, private believers with no corporate identity. But Christ established a visible body, a city set on a hill, a lamp on a stand. Public confession makes this visibility possible.

Fifth, public confession prepares us for eternity. Jesus promised to confess before the Father those who confess Him before men. Our present confession is connected to our future vindication. When we stand before the throne, Christ will acknowledge us as His own. He will say, "This one confessed Me. This one is Mine." What a glorious prospect, to be confessed by Christ before the Father and the angels! But this promise is for those who confess Him now. Present confession leads to future acknowledgment.

VII. The Ongoing Nature of Confession

Confession is not a one-time event but a lifelong practice. The initial confession at conversion is crucial. But confession must continue throughout our Christian journey. Paul exhorted Timothy:

> *"Fight the good fight of faith, lay hold on eternal life, to which you were also called and have confessed the good confession in the presence of many witnesses." (1 Timothy 6:12)*

Timothy had confessed the good confession. But Paul urged him to keep fighting, keep holding, keep confessing. The battle of faith continues. The confession must continue with it.

Paul himself modeled this ongoing confession:

> *"I have fought the good fight, I have finished the race, I have kept the faith." (2 Timothy 4:7)*

Paul kept the faith throughout his life. He confessed Christ in Jerusalem and in Rome. He confessed before Jewish councils and Roman governors. He confessed in prisons and palaces. He confessed until his dying breath. We are called to the same perseverance.

Hebrews repeatedly exhorts us to hold fast:

> "Let us hold fast the confession of our hope without wavering, for He who promised is faithful." (Hebrews 10:23)

Notice that we hold fast "without wavering." Our confession is not to be vacillating or uncertain. It is not to shift with cultural winds or personal circumstances. It is to be steady, consistent, unwavering. And notice the reason: "He who promised is faithful." We can hold fast because He holds us. We can remain faithful because He is faithful. Our confession rests not on our strength but on His faithfulness.

Peter exhorts believers:

> "But sanctify the Lord God in your hearts, and always be ready to give a defense to everyone who asks you a reason for the hope that is in you, with meekness and fear." (1 Peter 3:15)

We should always be ready to confess. Not just in formal religious settings. Not just when asked by fellow believers. But to everyone who asks a reason for our hope. This readiness requires preparation. We must know what we believe and why. We must be able to articulate our faith clearly. But notice also the manner: with meekness and fear. Our confession is not arrogant or combative. It is humble and reverent. We speak truth with grace. We confess Christ with Christlikeness.

VIII. Confession of Sin

Ongoing confession also includes confession of sin. When we fail, we must acknowledge it. When we fall, we must confess it. John writes:

> "If we confess our sins, He is faithful and just to forgive us our sins and to cleanse us from all unrighteousness." (1 John 1:9)

This promise is for Christians who have already confessed Christ. Even after conversion, we need ongoing confession of our failures. This is not confession unto salvation that has already occurred. This is confession unto restoration of fellowship. Sin disrupts our communion with God. Confession restores it. We confess our sins by agreeing with God about them. We acknowledge our failure. We receive His forgiveness. Then we rise to confess Christ anew with renewed courage and commitment.

James also speaks to this ongoing confession:

> *"Confess your trespasses to one another, and pray for one another, that you may be healed. The effective, fervent prayer of a righteous man avails much." (James 5:16)*

Notice that James adds another dimension: confession to one another. This horizontal confession complements our vertical confession to God. When we have sinned against a brother or sister, we must confess to them. When we struggle with besetting sins, we benefit from confessing to trusted believers who can pray for us. This is not confession to a priest for absolution. This is confession to brothers and sisters for support, accountability, and prayer.

Such confession takes humility. It requires vulnerability. It demands trust. But it brings healing. The Greek word for healed in James 5:16 is iaomai (ἰάομαι) which can refer to physical healing but also to spiritual and emotional restoration. When we bring our sins into the light through confession, healing follows. When we hide them in darkness, they fester and grow. Confession is the path to wholeness.

Greek: iaomai (ἰάομαι): to heal, to cure, to restore

David understood this principle. When he tried to hide his sin with Bathsheba, his soul withered:

> *"When I kept silent, my bones grew old through my groaning all the day long. For day and night Your hand was heavy upon me; my vitality was turned into the drought of summer." (Psalm 32:3-4)*

But when David confessed, restoration came:

> *"I acknowledged my sin to You, and my iniquity I have not hidden. I said, 'I will confess my transgressions to the LORD,' and You forgave the iniquity of my sin." (Psalm 32:5)*

The act of confession released him from the burden of guilt. The forgiveness of God refreshed his soul. This same experience awaits every Christian who will humble themselves and confess.

Let me address three groups specifically this morning.

First, to those who have never confessed Christ: Today is the day of salvation. You have heard the gospel. Perhaps you believe in your heart that Jesus is Lord. But salvation requires confession with your mouth. Will you take that step today? Will you publicly confess Jesus Christ as your Lord and Savior? The promise stands sure: *"Whoever confesses Me before men, him I will also confess before My Father who is in heaven"* (Matthew 10:32). Imagine it: Jesus Christ, the Son of God, speaking your name before the Father. Acknowledging you as one of His own. Claiming you as His blood-bought possession. All this awaits those who confess Him. Do not let fear hold you back. Do not let pride keep you silent. Do not let the praise of men outweigh the praise of God. Confess Christ today, and He will confess you throughout eternity.

Second, to those who have been secret disciples: Perhaps you believe in Jesus but have kept your faith hidden. Maybe you fear what family, friends, or colleagues might think. Maybe you have convinced yourself that private faith is sufficient. Remember Jesus' words: whoever confesses Me, I will confess; whoever denies Me, I will deny. Silence in the face of opportunity is a form of denial. Step into the light. Declare your allegiance to Christ. The freedom and joy that come from open confession far outweigh any temporary discomfort. You were not saved to be hidden. You were saved to shine. Let your light shine before men. Let your confession ring clear.

Third, to those who have confessed Christ but grown silent: Perhaps you once boldly proclaimed your faith but have become quiet. Maybe disappointment, hurt, or simple neglect has muted your testimony. Maybe the cares of this world have choked your confession. Perhaps someone responded negatively to your witness, and you withdrew in pain. Perhaps the busyness of life has crowded out the urgency of evangelism. Perhaps you have simply grown comfortable in Christian circles where confession seems unnecessary. But the world outside those circles desperately needs your witness. Return to your first love. Renew your confession. Let your light shine again before men. The church needs your voice. The world needs your witness. Your family needs your example. Your community needs your testimony. Your neighbors need to hear the name of Jesus from your lips. Your coworkers need to see Christ reflected in your life and hear Him proclaimed by your words. Do not let the enemy steal your confession. Do not let circumstances silence your praise. Open your mouth and declare what you know to be true: Jesus Christ is Lord!

Chapter Five
The Necessity of Baptism

"There is also an antitype which now saves us-baptism."
(1 Peter 3:21)

Introduction

In our study of God's plan of salvation, we have examined the foundational elements of hearing the gospel, believing its message, repenting, turning our direction, and confessing Jesus as Lord. Each of these responses flows naturally into the next, building upon a growing faith that demands expression. Today we arrive at a point of decisive action, the moment when faith becomes embodied, when the believer is united with Christ in the most intimate way imaginable. We come to the subject of baptism.

Few subjects in the religious world generate more controversy than baptism. Questions abound regarding its mode, its subjects, and especially its purpose. Is baptism merely a symbol of an inward grace already received? Is it an outward sign of church membership? Or does baptism occupy a more essential place in God's redemptive plan? To answer these questions, we must examine the testimony of Scripture with careful attention to the original languages and the rich Old Testament background that gives baptism its deepest meaning.

I. The Meaning of Baptism

The English word "baptism" is not a translation but a transliteration, a carrying over of the Greek letters into English characters. The Greek verb is baptizō (βαπτιζω), and its meaning is neither obscure nor disputed among Greek scholars. The term means "to dip, to immerse, to submerge, to plunge." The related noun baptisma (βάπτισμα) refers to the act of immersion itself.

Greek: baptizō (βαπτίζω): to dip, to immerse, to submerge, to plunge

Classical Greek literature employed baptizō consistently with this meaning. The historian Polybius used the word to describe ships that had been "submerged" or sunk. Plutarch employed it to describe a person "plunged" under water. The medical writer Nicander used the term for cucumbers "dipped" in a pickling solution. In every case, the word carries the essential idea of complete immersion, of one object being entirely enveloped by another.

This meaning is preserved in the New Testament usage. When John baptized in the Jordan River, he chose a location where "there was much water" (John 3:23). The text tells us that Jesus "came up from the water" (Mark 1:10), and that Philip and the Ethiopian eunuch "went down into the water" and "came up out of the water" (Acts 8:38-39). These descriptions are nonsensical if baptism involved anything other than immersion.

The theological significance of the mode becomes clear when we consider Paul's teaching in Romans 6. Here the apostle describes baptism as a burial with Christ:

> *"Or do you not know that as many of us as were baptized into Christ Jesus were baptized into His death? Therefore, we were buried with Him through baptism into death, that just as Christ was raised from the dead by the glory of the Father, even so we also should walk in newness of life." (Romans 6:3-4)*

The imagery is unmistakable. As Christ was buried in the tomb and raised to new life, so the believer is buried in the waters of baptism and raised to walk in newness of life. Sprinkling or pouring cannot convey this burial symbolism. Only immersion, the complete submersion of the believer beneath the water and the subsequent rising, pictures the death, burial, and resurrection of our Lord.

II. Old Testament Foundations

While the term "baptism" does not appear in the Old Testament, the concept of ritual immersion and the salvific use of water permeate the Hebrew Scriptures. Understanding these foundations illuminates why baptism holds such a central place in God's redemptive plan.

The Flood of Noah: Salvation Through Water

The apostle Peter explicitly connects baptism to the flood narrative:

> "...in the days of Noah, while the ark was being prepared, in which a few, that is, eight souls, were saved through water. There is also an antitype which now saves us-baptism (not the removal of the filth of the flesh, but the answer of a good conscience toward God), through the resurrection of Jesus Christ." (1 Peter 3:20-21)

Peter's language is striking. He identifies baptism as the antitypon (ἀντίτυπον), the "antitype" or corresponding reality, of Noah's salvation through water. The flood waters that destroyed the wicked also lifted Noah and his family to safety in the ark. In the same way, baptism marks a separation from the old world of sin and an entrance into the safety of Christ.

Greek: antitypon (ἀντίτυπον): antitype, corresponding reality, counterpart

Notice that Peter emphatically states baptism "now saves us." He immediately clarifies that this salvation does not come from the mere physical washing, "not the removal of the filth of the flesh," but from what baptism represents: "the answer of a good conscience toward God."

The Greek word eperōtēma (ἐπερώτημα), translated "answer," can also mean "pledge" or "appeal." Baptism is the pledge of a purified conscience, the appeal of faith reaching out to appropriate God's grace through the resurrection of Jesus Christ.

Greek: eperōtēma (ἐπερώτημα): answer, pledge, appeal

The Red Sea Crossing: Baptism into Moses

Paul draws another explicit connection between Old Testament water events and Christian baptism:

> *"Moreover, brethren, I do not want you to be unaware that all our fathers were under the cloud, all passed through the sea, all were baptized into Moses in the cloud and in the sea." (1 Corinthians 10:1-2)*

The Hebrew term for the Red Sea is yam suph (יַם־סוּף), meaning "Sea of Reeds" or "Sea of the End," a name pregnant with theological meaning. At this sea, Egypt's power came to an end; Israel's bondage came to an end; the old life came to an end. Through the waters, Israel emerged as a nation in covenant relationship with God, "baptized into Moses."

Hebrew: yam suph (יַם־סוּף): Sea of Reeds, Sea of the End (the Red Sea)

The parallels to Christian baptism are substantive. As Israel was delivered from Egyptian bondage through water, believers are delivered from the bondage of sin through baptism. As Israel emerged on the other side as God's covenant people, believers emerge from baptism as members of Christ's body, the church. As there was no other way for Israel to reach the Promised Land except through the sea, there is no other way to enter the kingdom except through the waters of baptism.

Naaman the Syrian: Cleansing Through Obedience

The account of Naaman in 2 Kings 5 provides another powerful illustration. Naaman, commander of the Syrian army, suffered from leprosy, a condition that rendered him ceremonially unclean. The prophet Elisha instructed him:

> *"Go and wash in the Jordan seven times, and your flesh shall be restored to you, and you shall be clean." (2 Kings 5:10)*

Naaman's initial reaction reveals a mindset common to many who resist baptism today. He was angry. He expected the prophet to perform some dramatic act. He noted that the rivers of Damascus were surely superior to the muddy Jordan. Why should the particular waters matter? Why should the specific action be necessary?

The Hebrew verb used for Naaman's commanded washing is rachats (רָחַץ), meaning "to wash, to bathe." But when the text describes what Naaman actually did, it employs a different term: vayyitbol (וַיִּטְבֹּל), from the root taval (טָבַל), meaning "to dip, to immerse." This is the Hebrew equivalent of the Greek baptizō. Naaman immersed himself seven times in the Jordan, and his flesh was restored "like the flesh of a little child."

> *Hebrew: taval (טָבַל): to dip, to immerse (Hebrew equivalent of Greek baptizō)*

The lesson is clear: God's blessings come through obedient faith, not through human reasoning about what ought to be sufficient. Naaman was not healed by the water of the Jordan; he was healed by God's power appropriated through obedient faith. Yet had he refused to dip himself in the Jordan, he would have remained a leper. So too with baptism: the power to save is not in the water itself, but in the blood of Christ contacted through obedient faith.

The Mikveh: Ritual Immersion in Jewish Practice

The Jewish practice of ritual immersion, centered on the mikveh (מִקְוֶה), provides essential background for understanding New Testament baptism. The mikveh was a pool of water used for ritual purification, required for priests before serving in the temple, for those cleansed from various forms of uncleanness, and for Gentile converts to Judaism.

The term mikveh appears in Leviticus 11:36, where it refers to a "gathering" or "collection" of water. The word shares its root with tikvah (תִּקְוָה), meaning "hope." This linguistic connection is meaningful: the gathering of waters became a place of hope, a point of transition from impurity to purity, from exclusion to inclusion in the covenant community.

> Hebrew: mikveh (מִקְוֶה): gathering of water, ritual immersion pool; related to tikvah (hope)

When John the Baptist appeared preaching a "baptism of repentance for the remission of sins" (Mark 1:4), his Jewish audience would have immediately understood the symbolism. Immersion marked transition. Immersion marked purification. Immersion marked a new beginning. John's baptism called Israel to prepare for the coming Messiah through repentance expressed in immersion.

III. The Laver of the Tabernacle

The Tabernacle of Moses provides another striking Old Testament type that illuminates the necessity of baptism. God gave Moses precise instructions for constructing this sacred tent where His presence would dwell among Israel. Every element of its design carried spiritual significance, and the book of Hebrews confirms that these earthly shadows pointed to heavenly realities fulfilled in Christ and His church.

Between the bronze altar of sacrifice and the entrance to the Holy Place stood the kiyyor (כִּיּוֹר), the bronze laver or basin filled with water. This placement was theologically significant: after the sacrifice was offered at the altar, but before the priest could enter God's presence in the Holy Place, he was required to wash.

> Hebrew: kiyyor (כִּיּוֹר): laver, basin (the bronze washbasin in the Tabernacle)

> *"For Aaron and his sons shall wash their hands and their feet in water from it. When they go into the tabernacle of meeting, or when they come near the altar to minister, to burn an offering made by fire to the LORD, they shall wash with water, lest they die. So they shall wash their hands and their feet, lest they die. And it shall be a statute forever to them-to him and his descendants throughout their generations." (Exodus 30:19-21)*

The command is emphatic: wash, lest they die. No priest, regardless of his lineage or sincerity, could bypass the laver and enter the Holy Place. The washing was not optional. It was not merely symbolic of a cleansing that had already occurred. It was the required means of preparation for entering God's presence.

The Hebrew verb used here is rachats (רָחַץ), meaning "to wash, to bathe." This is the same word used when Elisha commanded Naaman to wash in the Jordan.

The laver itself was made from the bronze mirrors of the women who served at the entrance of the Tabernacle (Exodus 38:8), suggesting that the washing involved not only cleansing but also self-examination, seeing oneself truly before approaching a holy God.

The typological significance becomes clear when we recognize what the Tabernacle represented. The writer of Hebrews explains that the earthly Tabernacle was "a copy and shadow of the heavenly things" (Hebrews 8:5). The sacrifices, the priesthood, the furniture, all pointed forward to Christ and the realities of the new covenant.

If the Tabernacle was a type, what is its antitype?

> *"But Christ came as High Priest of the good things to come, with the greater and more perfect tabernacle not made with hands, that is, not of this creation. Not with the blood of goats and calves, but with His own blood He entered the Most Holy Place once for all, having obtained eternal redemption." (Hebrews 9:11-12)*

Christ is our High Priest. His blood is the sacrifice offered once for all. And the church, His body, is the spiritual house where God now dwells:

> *"You also, as living stones, are being built up a spiritual house, a holy priesthood, to offer up spiritual sacrifices acceptable to God through Jesus Christ." (1 Peter 2:5)*

Under the new covenant, all Christians are priests with access to God's presence. But just as the Levitical priests could not enter the Tabernacle without washing at the laver, we cannot enter the church, the spiritual dwelling place of God, without the washing of baptism. The pattern established in the type demands fulfillment in the antitype.

> *"Let us draw near with a true heart in full assurance of faith, having our hearts sprinkled from an evil conscience and our bodies washed with pure water." (Hebrews 10:22)*

The writer of Hebrews draws this very connection. The "bodies washed with pure water" is a clear reference to baptism, paralleling the washing that preceded entrance into God's presence under the old covenant. This washing is not ceremonial formality but the appointed means by which we draw near to God with cleansed hearts and consciences.

The progression in the Tabernacle was fixed and inviolable: altar, then laver, then Holy Place. No priest could rearrange the order or skip a step. In the same way, the progression in God's plan of salvation follows a divine order: the blood of Christ is applied to the penitent believer in the waters of baptism, and through that washing, the believer enters the church where God's presence dwells. To claim entrance without the washing is to approach God on our own terms rather than His, and under the old covenant, such presumption brought death.

The laver stood as a perpetual reminder that sinful humanity cannot approach a holy God without cleansing. That truth has not changed. What has changed is the nature of the cleansing: no longer the repeated washings of an earthly priesthood, but the once-for-all washing of baptism into Christ, where His blood cleanses us from all sin and grants us access to the Father forevermore.

IV. The Purpose of Baptism

With this Old Testament background in mind, we can better appreciate the New Testament's teaching on baptism's purpose. The Scriptures consistently present baptism not as an optional symbol for those already saved, but as an essential response of faith through which God's saving grace is received.

For the Remission of Sins

On the day of Pentecost, when the crowd was convicted by Peter's proclamation that they had crucified the Lord of glory, they cried out, "Men and brethren, what shall we do?" Peter's response was immediate and unambiguous:

> *"Repent, and let every one of you be baptized in the name of Jesus Christ for the remission of sins; and you shall receive the gift of the Holy Spirit." (Acts 2:38)*

The Greek phrase eis aphesin hamartiōn (εἰς ἄφεσιν ἁμαρτιῶν), translated "for the remission of sins," is grammatically decisive. The preposition eis (εἰς) with the accusative case indicates purpose or result: "unto," "into," "in order to obtain." This is the same construction used when Jesus said His blood was shed "for the remission of sins" (Matthew 26:28). No one argues that Christ's blood was shed "because sins had already been forgiven." Similarly, baptism is "for the remission of sins": that is, in order to obtain that forgiveness.

The word aphesis (ἄφεσις) means "release, pardon, cancellation of an obligation." It derives from aphiēmi (ἀφίημι), "to send away, to let go." In baptism, sins are "sent away"; the guilt is released; the debt is cancelled. This is not the result of the physical water, but of Christ's blood applied to the penitent believer at the point of their obedient immersion.

Greek: aphesis (ἄφεσις): release, pardon, remission, cancellation of an obligation

To Wash Away Sins

When the Lord appeared to Saul on the Damascus road, Saul believed and spent three days in fasting and prayer. Yet he remained in his sins until Ananias came with this instruction:

> *"And now why are you waiting? Arise and be baptized, and wash away your sins, calling on the name of the Lord." (Acts 22:16)*

The verb apolousai (ἀπόλουσαι) means "to wash off, to wash away completely." It is an aorist middle imperative, a command requiring Saul's own participation in an action to be completed at a definite point. Saul's sins were not washed away during his three days of prayer and fasting. They were washed away when he arose and was baptized, calling on the Lord's name in that act of faith.

Greek: apolousai (ἀπόλουσαι): to wash off, to wash away completely

Notice the present participle epikalesamenos (ἐπικαλεσάμενος), "calling on." Baptism is itself a calling upon the Lord's name, an appeal to God for salvation based on Christ's finished work. This confirms Peter's language that baptism is "the answer of a good conscience toward God" (1 Peter 3:21).

To Be Clothed with Christ

Paul's letter to the Galatians contains another crucial statement about baptism's purpose:

> *"For you are all sons of God through faith in Christ Jesus. For as many of you as were baptized into Christ have put on Christ." (Galatians 3:26-27)*

The phrase "baptized into Christ" (eis Christon ebaptisthēte, εἰς Χριστὸν ἐβαπτίσθητε) describes movement from outside to inside: from being without Christ to being "in Christ." It is through baptism that this transition occurs.

The verb "put on" (enedysasthe, ἐνεδύσασθε) was commonly used for putting on a garment. When one emerges from the waters of baptism, they are clothed with Christ Himself. All that Christ is, His righteousness, His relationship with the Father, His inheritance, becomes the possession of the baptized believer. We stand before God not in our own filthy rags, but robed in Christ's perfect righteousness.

To Enter the Body of Christ

Paul further teaches that baptism is the means of entry into Christ's body, the church:

> *"For by one Spirit we were all baptized into one body-whether Jews or Greeks, whether slaves or free-and have all been made to drink into one Spirit." (1 Corinthians 12:13)*

The church is described in Scripture as Christ's body, and salvation is "in Christ." If baptism is the means of entering the body, and the body is where the saved are, then baptism is essential to salvation. One cannot be in Christ without being in His body, and one enters His body through baptism.

V. The Commission of Christ

The Lord's final commission to His apostles includes baptism as an essential component:

> *"Go into all the world and preach the gospel to every creature. He who believes and is baptized will be saved; but he who does not believe will be condemned." (Mark 16:15-16)*

Jesus places belief and baptism together as the conditions for salvation. Some object that the latter clause only mentions unbelief as the cause of condemnation. But this is precisely what we would expect: one who does not believe would never submit to baptism, making it unnecessary to mention. The absence of a statement is not a denial of its truth. Jesus did not say, "He who believes and is not baptized will be saved." What He did say is clear: "He who believes and is baptized will be saved."

> *"Go therefore and make disciples of all the nations, baptizing them in the name of the Father and of the Son and of the Holy Spirit, teaching them to observe all things that I have commanded you." (Matthew 28:19-20)*

The Great Commission presents baptism as integral to disciple-making. The main verb "make disciples" (mathēteusate, μαθητεύσατε) is accomplished through the participles "baptizing" (baptizontes, βαπτίζοντες) and "teaching" (didaskontes, διδάσκοντες). One becomes a disciple through being baptized and taught. These are not optional additions but essential components of the disciple-making process.

VI. The Meaning of Our Immersion

We return to Romans 6, where Paul develops the richest theology of baptism found anywhere in Scripture:

> *"Or do you not know that as many of us as were baptized into Christ Jesus were baptized into His death? Therefore we were buried with Him through baptism into death, that just as Christ was raised from the dead by the glory of the Father, even so we also should walk in newness of life. For if we have been united together in the likeness of His death, certainly we also shall be in the likeness of His resurrection, knowing this, that our old man was crucified with Him, that the body of sin might be done away with, that we should no longer be slaves of sin. For he who has died has been freed from sin." (Romans 6:3-7)*

Paul's argument hinges on union with Christ. Through baptism, we are joined to Christ in His death, burial, and resurrection. The "old man," our former life of sin, is crucified with Christ. We are "buried with Him through baptism into death." We are raised to "walk in newness of life."

The term "united together" (symphytoi, σύμφυτοι) literally means "grown together, planted together." It suggests an organic union, like a branch grafted into a tree. Through baptism, we become one with Christ; His death becomes our death to sin; His resurrection becomes our resurrection to new life.

Greek: symphytoi (σύμφυτοι): grown together, planted together, united organically

Paul repeats this teaching to the Colossians:

"buried with Him in baptism, in which you also were raised with Him through faith in the working of God, who raised Him from the dead. And you, being dead in your trespasses and the uncircumcision of your flesh, He has made alive together with Him, having forgiven you all trespasses." (Colossians 2:12-13)

Notice the phrase "through faith in the working of God" (dia tēs pisteōs tēs energeias tou theou, διὰ τῆς πίστεως τῆς ἐνεργείας τοῦ θεοῦ). Baptism is not a work of human merit; it is an act of faith in God's powerful working. Just as God raised Christ from the dead, so God raises the believer from the waters of baptism to new life. The power is God's; the faith that accesses that power is expressed in baptism.

VII. Objections Considered

"We Are Saved by Grace, Not Works"

This is absolutely true. Ephesians 2:8-9 clearly states that salvation is by grace through faith, not of works. But baptism is not a meritorious work by which we earn salvation. It is an act of faith through which we receive the gift that grace offers.

Consider Naaman again. Was he healed by his own work of dipping in the Jordan? No, he was healed by God's power. But that power was accessed through obedient faith expressed in the commanded action. Consider the Israelites at Jericho. Did they conquer the city by their own might in marching around it? No, God gave them the victory. But they had to march in obedient faith.

Baptism stands in the same relationship to salvation. We are saved by Christ's blood, not by water. But we contact that blood through the obedience of faith, just as the Israelites under Moses contacted God's deliverance by passing through the sea, just as the Israelites under Joshua contacted God's victory by marching around Jericho.

"The Thief on the Cross Was Saved Without Baptism"

The thief on the cross lived and died under the old covenant. Jesus had authority on earth to forgive sins directly (Matthew 9:6). The New Testament, with its specific commands regarding baptism, did not take effect until after Christ's death:

> "For where there is a testament, there must also of necessity be the death of the testator. For a testament is in force after men are dead, since it has no power at all while the testator lives." (Hebrews 9:16-17)

The thief was saved under the dispensation in which he lived, just as countless Old Testament saints were saved without Christian baptism. But we live under the new covenant, and under this covenant, baptism is commanded for the remission of sins. We cannot reach back to a different dispensation to justify disobedience to our Lord's commands.

"We Are Justified by Faith Alone"

The phrase "faith alone" appears only once in Scripture, in James 2:24, where it is explicitly denied: "You see then that a man is justified by works, and not by faith alone." The "works" James describes are not meritorious works of the Law but the obedient expression of genuine faith.

Abraham believed God, and it was counted to him for righteousness (Genesis 15:6). But when was this belief perfected? James answers: *"Was not Abraham our father justified by works when he offered Isaac his son on the altar? Do you see that faith was working together with his works, and by works faith was made perfect?"* (James 2:21-22).

Faith that does not express itself in obedience is dead faith, and dead faith cannot save (James 2:17, 26). Living faith acts upon God's commands. When God says to be baptized for the remission of sins, living faith responds in obedience.

VIII. The Urgency of Response

In every New Testament conversion account, baptism occurs immediately upon belief. On Pentecost, three thousand were baptized "that day" (Acts 2:41). The Ethiopian eunuch was baptized beside the road the moment he believed (Acts 8:36-38). The Philippian jailer and his household were baptized "the same hour of the night" (Acts 16:33). Saul was told, "Why are you waiting?" (Acts 22:16).

There was no waiting period. There was no probationary membership. There was no "accepting Jesus" followed months later by baptism. The urgency of baptism in the apostolic church reflects its essential nature. One does not delay what is necessary for salvation.

If you have heard the gospel and believed its message, if you have confessed Jesus as Lord, then one step remains. Like Naaman at the Jordan, like Israel at the sea, like the Pentecost believers on that historic day, you are called to be buried with Christ in baptism and raised to walk in newness of life.

Why are you waiting? The same Lord who shed His blood for your sins commands you to be baptized. The same grace that offers salvation provides the means to receive it. The same faith that believes in Christ expresses itself in obedience to Christ.

Today, if you will hear His voice, do not harden your heart. Arise, and be baptized, and wash away your sins, calling on the name of the Lord.

82

Chapter Six
Walking in Holiness

"I beseech you therefore, brethren, by the mercies of God, that you present your bodies a living sacrifice, holy, acceptable to God, which is your reasonable service." (Romans 12:1)

Introduction

Throughout this series on God's plan of salvation, we have traced the journey of the soul from darkness into light. We began with the hearing of the gospel, that powerful message of Christ's death, burial, and resurrection that reaches the ears and penetrates the heart. We examined the response of faith, that trust in God's promises that moves beyond mere intellectual assent to wholehearted commitment. We discussed repentance, that turning away from sin and toward God that marks the genuine change of heart and direction. We considered the confession of Jesus as Lord, that public declaration that identifies us with Christ before the world. And we concluded with baptism, that burial with Christ in water through which we contact His saving blood and rise to walk in newness of life.

But what is this "newness of life" into which we have risen? What does it mean to walk as a child of God? Having been saved by grace through faith, how then shall we live? These are not peripheral questions for the curious but essential matters for every believer.

The same apostle who declared that we are saved by grace apart from works of the law also insisted that we are "created in Christ Jesus for good works, which God prepared beforehand that we should walk in them" (Ephesians 2:10). Salvation is not merely rescue from something; it is transformation into something. We have been called out of darkness into marvelous light, and those who walk in the light do not continue in the patterns of darkness.

The apostle Paul, having spent eleven chapters in his epistle to the Romans expounding the riches of God's mercy in the gospel, now turns to the practical implications of that gospel for daily living. His transition is marked by that significant word "therefore." Because of all that God has done for us in Christ, because of the mercies lavished upon undeserving sinners, because of justification by faith and peace with God and hope of glory, therefore we are called to respond with the totality of our being. The proper response to grace is not passivity but consecration, not continued sinning that grace may abound but the offering of ourselves as living sacrifices to the God who has redeemed us.

I. The Call to Holiness: Understanding What God Requires

Before we can pursue holiness, we must understand what holiness means. The term is used so frequently in religious discourse that it can become emptied of its content, reduced to a vague notion of moral goodness or religious piety. But the biblical concept of holiness is far richer and more demanding than such diluted understandings suggest.

The primary Hebrew word for holy is qadosh (קָדוֹשׁ), and its fundamental meaning is "set apart, separated, distinct." When applied to God, it speaks of His utter transcendence, His complete otherness from everything created. God is not merely greater than we are in degree; He is different from us in kind. He is wholly other, dwelling in unapproachable light, high and lifted up, before whom even the seraphim cover their faces and cry:

> *"Holy, holy, holy is the LORD of hosts; the whole earth is full of His glory!" (Isaiah 6:3)*
>
> *Hebrew: qadosh (קָדוֹשׁ): set apart, separated, distinct, holy*

The threefold repetition of "holy" is significant. In Hebrew, repetition indicates emphasis and intensity. To say something twice is to stress its importance. To say it three times is to express the superlative degree, the highest possible intensity. God is not merely holy, not merely most holy, but holy, holy, holy. His holiness is infinite, absolute, and incomparable. There is none like Him in all creation.

When this holiness is extended to persons, places, or objects, it means that they have been set apart from common use for sacred purposes. The Sabbath was holy because it was set apart from the other days for rest and worship. The tabernacle was holy because it was set apart from other structures as the dwelling place of God. The priests were holy because they were set apart from the other tribes to serve before the Lord. And Israel as a nation was called to be holy because they were set apart from all other peoples to belong to God in a special covenant relationship.

> *"Speak to all the congregation of the children of Israel, and say to them: 'You shall be holy, for I the LORD your God am holy.'" (Leviticus 19:2)*

This command establishes the foundation of biblical holiness. The call to be holy is not an arbitrary requirement but a reflection of God's own character. Because God is holy, His people must be holy. The relationship between Creator and creature, between Redeemer and redeemed, demands correspondence of character. Those who belong to the Holy One must themselves be set apart, distinct from the patterns of the world around them.

> *"Consecrate yourselves therefore, and be holy, for I am the LORD your God. And you shall keep My statutes, and perform them: I am the LORD who sanctifies you." (Leviticus 20:7-8)*

The verb "consecrate" is hitqaddishthem (הִתְקַדִּשְׁתֶּם), the reflexive form of the root qadash, meaning "to make oneself holy, to set oneself apart." There is human responsibility in holiness. We must actively consecrate ourselves. Yet the verse concludes with the reminder that it is ultimately the Lord who sanctifies. Holiness is both a command to be obeyed and a gift to be received, both our work and God's work in us.

The New Testament employs the Greek word hagios (ἅγιος) to translate the Hebrew qadosh. The term carries the same essential meaning of separation and consecration. Believers are called hagioi (ἅγιοι), "saints" or "holy ones," not because of their moral perfection but because of their position in Christ. They have been set apart by God for His purposes. The related noun hagiasmos (ἁγιασμός) is typically translated "sanctification" or "holiness" and refers to the process by which believers are made holy in practice as well as in position.

Greek: hagios (ἅγιος): holy, set apart, sacred; hagiasmos (ἁγιασμός) - sanctification

Peter draws explicitly on the Levitical command when he writes:

"As obedient children, not conforming yourselves to the former lusts, as in your ignorance; but as He who called you is holy, you also be holy in all your conduct, because it is written, 'Be holy, for I am holy.'" (1 Peter 1:14-16)

The apostle makes clear that the Old Testament command to holiness has not been abolished but has been extended to all who are in Christ. The standard remains the same: the holiness of God Himself. The motivation remains the same: we are to be holy because He is holy. What has changed is the scope of the covenant community. Now Jew and Gentile alike, all who have been born again through the living word of God, are called to this holy manner of life.

The writer of Hebrews emphasizes the essential nature of this holiness:

"Pursue peace with all people, and holiness, without which no one will see the Lord." (Hebrews 12:14)

The verb "pursue" is diōkete (διώκετε), a strong word meaning "to chase after, to pursue eagerly, to press toward."

Holiness is not a passive state into which we drift but an active pursuit that requires intentional effort. And the stakes could not be higher: without holiness, no one will see the Lord. This is not salvation by works, for we have already established that salvation comes by grace through faith. But it is the insistence that genuine faith produces genuine transformation. Those who have truly been saved will pursue the holiness that characterizes their Savior.

Greek: diōkete (διώκετε): to chase after, to pursue eagerly, to press toward

II. The Living Sacrifice: Understanding Romans 12:1

Having established the biblical foundation for the call to holiness, we now turn to our primary text, where Paul provides the paradigm for holy living in the new covenant:

> "I beseech you therefore, brethren, by the mercies of God, that you present your bodies a living sacrifice, holy, acceptable to God, which is your reasonable service." (Romans 12:1)

Paul's appeal is grounded not in law but in grace. He does not command but beseeches. He does not threaten but appeals "by the mercies of God." The word "mercies" is oiktirmōn (οἰκτιρμῶν), a term that speaks of deep compassion, of bowels moved with pity. It is the plural form, suggesting the manifold expressions of God's compassion toward sinners.

Greek: oiktirmōn (οἰκτιρμῶν): mercies, deep compassion, tender feelings of pity

What are these mercies? They are everything Paul has expounded in the preceding eleven chapters. The mercy of justification by faith, through which guilty sinners are declared righteous before God. The mercy of peace with God, through which those who were enemies have been reconciled. The mercy of access into grace, through which we now stand in God's favor. The mercy of hope, through which we await the glory yet to be revealed. The mercy of the Spirit, through whom God's love has been poured out in our hearts. The mercy of Christ's death for us while we were still sinners. The mercy of deliverance from the law of sin and death. The mercy of adoption as children and heirs of God. The mercy of divine preservation, through which nothing can separate us from God's love.

These mercies are the foundation of the Christian life. We do not pursue holiness to earn God's favor; we pursue holiness because we have already received His favor. We do not offer ourselves to God in hopes that He will accept us; we offer ourselves because He has already accepted us in the Beloved. Grace precedes obedience, and gratitude is the engine of sanctification. As the hymn writer expressed it, "Love so amazing, so divine, demands my soul, my life, my all."

The verb "present" is parastēsai (παραστῆσαι), an aorist infinitive suggesting a decisive, once-for-all action. It is the same word used in Romans 6:13 where Paul exhorts believers to present their members as instruments of righteousness. The term was used in sacrificial contexts for the offering of an animal to be sacrificed, and this sacrificial imagery permeates Paul's instruction.

> *Greek: parastēsai (παραστῆσαι): to present, to offer, to place beside (sacrificial term)*

Notice that Paul specifies "your bodies." Christianity is not a religion of disembodied spirituality. The body matters. What we do with our physical selves has spiritual significance. Our hands, our feet, our eyes, our tongues, our appetites, our physical presence in the world - all of these are to be offered to God. The ancient Gnostic heresy that denigrated the body as inherently evil has no place in biblical faith. The body that God created, the body that Christ assumed in the incarnation - that body is to be presented as an offering to God.

"Or do you not know that your body is the temple of the Holy Spirit who is in you, whom you have from God, and you are not your own? For you were bought at a price; therefore, glorify God in your body and in your spirit, which are God's." (1 Corinthians 6:19-20)

The body of the believer is sacred space, the dwelling place of the Holy Spirit. Just as the temple in Jerusalem was consecrated for God's presence, so our physical bodies have been set apart for His habitation. This reality has implications for how we treat our bodies and what we do with them. Sexual immorality, drunkenness, gluttony, laziness, and all forms of bodily abuse are incompatible with the body's status as God's temple.

The phrase "living sacrifice" (thysian zōsan, θυσίαν ζῶσαν) would have struck Paul's readers as paradoxical. In the Old Testament sacrificial system, animals were killed before being offered. The sacrifice died so that the worshiper might live. But now Paul speaks of a sacrifice that remains alive, a sacrifice that continues to breathe and move and act in the world.

Greek: thysian zōsan (θυσίαν ζῶσαν): a living sacrifice

This living sacrifice represents the totality of Christian existence. We do not merely give God a portion of our time or a percentage of our resources; we give Him ourselves. Every moment is sacred. Every activity is worship. Every choice is an offering. The entire life of the believer, from waking to sleeping, from work to rest, from eating to fasting, becomes an act of consecration to God.

The Old Testament provided a glimpse of this concept in the whole burnt offering, the olah (עֹלָה), which was completely consumed on the altar. Unlike the peace offerings where the worshiper ate a portion, the burnt offering went up entirely to God as a sweet aroma. It represented total consecration, complete surrender. The living sacrifice of Romans 12:1 is the new covenant equivalent: a life wholly given to God, with nothing held back, nothing reserved for selfish purposes.

> *Hebrew: olah (עֹלָה): whole burnt offering, ascending offering (entirely consumed on the altar)*

Paul describes this living sacrifice with two adjectives. First, it must be "holy" (hagian, ἁγίαν). The sacrifice we offer must correspond to the character of the God to whom we offer it. Under the old covenant, sacrificial animals had to be without blemish. A lame or sick animal was an insult to God, not an act of worship. In the same way, we cannot offer God the scraps of our lives while reserving the best for ourselves. The living sacrifice must be holy, set apart, consecrated, pure.

Second, the sacrifice must be "acceptable to God" (euareston tō theō, εὐάρεστον τῷ θεῷ). The word euarestos means "well-pleasing, agreeable." It is possible to offer sacrifices that God does not accept. The prophets frequently condemned Israel for their hypocritical worship, their sacrifices offered with unrepentant hearts and unchanged lives.

> *Greek: euarestos (εὐάρεστος): well-pleasing, acceptable, agreeable*

> *"To what purpose is the multitude of your sacrifices to Me?" says the LORD. "I have had enough of burnt offerings of rams and the fat of fed cattle. I do not delight in the blood of bulls, or of lambs or goats. When you come to appear before Me, who has required this from your hand, to trample My courts? Bring no more futile sacrifices; incense is an abomination to Me." (Isaiah 1:11-13)*

God is not impressed by religious activity divorced from righteous living. The sacrifice He desires is a life conformed to His will, a heart that loves what He loves and hates what He hates. Samuel's rebuke to Saul echoes across the centuries: *"Has the LORD as great delight in burnt offerings and sacrifices, as in obeying the voice of the LORD? Behold, to obey is better than sacrifice, and to heed than the fat of rams"* (1 Samuel 15:22).

Paul concludes by designating this living sacrifice as our "reasonable service." The Greek phrase is tēn logikēn latreian hymōn (τὴν λογικὴν λατρείαν ὑμῶν). The term latreia refers to sacred service, particularly the service rendered by the Levitical priests in the tabernacle and temple. Paul is saying that all believers now serve as priests, and our priestly service is the offering of our very lives.

> *Greek: latreia (λατρεία): sacred service, priestly ministry, worship*

The adjective logikēn (from which we get "logical") can be translated "reasonable," "rational," or "spiritual." Some translations render it "spiritual worship," emphasizing the contrast with the physical sacrifices of the old covenant. Others translate it "reasonable service," emphasizing that this is the only fitting response to God's mercies. Both nuances are likely present. In light of all that God has done for us, offering ourselves completely to Him is the only rational, logical, reasonable response. Anything less would be ingratitude; anything less would be madness.

III. The Transformed Mind: The Key to Holy Living

Having called for the presentation of our bodies, Paul immediately turns to the transformation of our minds. The two are inseparable. What we do with our bodies flows from what we think in our minds. Holy living requires holy thinking.

> *"And do not be conformed to this world, but be transformed by the renewing of your mind, that you may prove what is that good and acceptable and perfect will of God." (Romans 12:2)*

The verb "conformed" is syschēmatizesthe (συσχηματίζεσθε), from the root schēma, meaning "outward form, fashion, appearance." It describes an external conformity to a pattern or mold. Paul commands believers not to allow themselves to be pressed into the mold of "this world" (tō aiōni toutō, τῷ αἰῶνι τούτῳ), literally "this age."

> *Greek: syschēmatizesthe (συσχηματίζεσθε): to be conformed to, to be pressed into a mold*

"This age" refers to the Mosaic age that was passing away as Paul wrote. The old covenant, with its sacrifices and ceremonies, its temple and priesthood, was drawing to its ordained close. Within a few short years, Jerusalem would fall, the temple would be destroyed, and the entire sacrificial system would come to a visible and violent end. Paul urges believers not to be conformed to the patterns of that fading age but to embrace the new covenant realities that had dawned in Christ. The law had served its purpose as a tutor to bring Israel to the Messiah, but now that faith had come, they were no longer under that tutor. To cling to the shadows when the substance had arrived, to return to the types when the antitype stood before them, was to be conformed to an age that God Himself was bringing to a close.

For us today, the world has its own wisdom, but it is foolishness before God. The world has its own standards of success, but they are measured by wealth and power and prestige rather than by faithfulness and service and humility. The world has its own pleasures, but they are fleeting and ultimately empty.

The pressure to conform is relentless. From childhood, we are shaped by the culture around us. Its values are absorbed through education, entertainment, advertising, and social expectation. We learn to want what the world tells us to want, to admire what the world tells us to admire, to fear what the world tells us to fear. Without conscious resistance, we will inevitably be squeezed into the world's mold.

> *"Adulterers and adulteresses! Do you not know that friendship with the world is enmity with God? Whoever therefore wants to be a friend of the world makes himself an enemy of God." (James 4:4)*

The language is deliberately strong. Friendship with the world is spiritual adultery, a betrayal of our covenant relationship with God. We cannot serve two masters. We cannot embrace both the values of the kingdom and the values of the age.

> *"Do not love the world or the things in the world. If anyone loves the world, the love of the Father is not in him. For all that is in the world-the lust of the flesh, the lust of the eyes, and the pride of life-is not of the Father but is of the world. And the world is passing away, and the lust of it; but he who does the will of God abides forever." (1 John 2:15-17)*

John identifies three categories that characterize worldliness: the lust of the flesh (physical appetites demanding gratification), the lust of the eyes (covetous desire for what we see), and the pride of life (boastful arrogance about possessions and achievements). These three correspond to the temptation of Eve in the garden, who saw that the tree was good for food (lust of the flesh), pleasant to the eyes (lust of the eyes), and desirable to make one wise (pride of life). They also correspond to Satan's temptation of Jesus in the wilderness. The patterns of the world are ancient, and they must be consciously rejected.

Against the negative command stands the positive: "be transformed." The verb is metamorphousthe (μεταμορφοῦσθε), from which we derive the English word "metamorphosis." Unlike schēma, which refers to outward form, morphē refers to essential form, the inner reality that determines outward expression. The transformation Paul envisions is not merely behavioral modification but fundamental change at the deepest level of our being.

> *Greek: metamorphousthe (μεταμορφοῦσθε): to be transformed, to undergo metamorphosis*

This is the word used to describe Christ's transfiguration on the mountain, when His inner glory broke through the veil of His humanity and His face shone like the sun. It is the word used in 2 Corinthians 3:18 to describe the progressive transformation of believers into the image of Christ: "But we all, with unveiled face, beholding as in a mirror the glory of the Lord, are being transformed into the same image from glory to glory, just as by the Spirit of the Lord."

The transformation takes place "by the renewing of your mind." The noun "renewing" (anakainōsei, ἀνακαινώσει) refers to a renovation, a making new again. The mind that was darkened by sin, corrupted by the fall, and shaped by the patterns of the world is progressively renewed by the work of the Holy Spirit through the word of God.

> *Greek: anakainōsei (ἀνακαινώσει): renewal, renovation, making new again*
>
> *"that you put off, concerning your former conduct, the old man which grows corrupt according to the deceitful lusts, and be renewed in the spirit of your mind, and that you put on the new man which was created according to God, in true righteousness and holiness." (Ephesians 4:22-24)*

The imagery is of changing clothes. The old garments of the former life, stained and corrupted by sin, are removed. New garments are put on, garments characterized by righteousness and holiness. But this change of clothing requires the renewal of the mind. We must learn to think differently before we can live differently. The patterns of thought that characterized the old life must be replaced with patterns of thought that reflect the character of God.

This is why the intake of Scripture is so essential to holy living. The psalmist asked, "How can a young man cleanse his way?" and answered, "By taking heed according to Your word" (Psalm 119:9). He declared, *"Your word I have hidden in my heart, that I might not sin against You"* (Psalm 119:11). The word of God renews the mind by replacing worldly thinking with divine truth. As we meditate on Scripture, memorize its teachings, and apply its principles, our minds are progressively transformed.

The purpose of this transformation is "that you may prove what is that good and acceptable and perfect will of God." The verb "prove" (dokimazein, δοκιμάζειν) means "to test, to examine, to approve after testing." A renewed mind is able to discern God's will, to test various courses of action and recognize which ones align with His purposes. The world-conformed mind cannot discern God's will because it operates according to different values and priorities. But the transformed mind, renewed by the Spirit and shaped by the word, develops spiritual discernment. It learns to recognize what is good (beneficial, advantageous), what is acceptable (well-pleasing to God), and what is perfect (complete, fully aligned with God's purposes).

> *Greek: dokimazein (δοκιμάζειν): to test, to examine, to approve after testing, to discern*

IV. Practical Holiness: What the Living Sacrifice Looks Like

The remainder of Romans 12 and the following chapters provide concrete examples of what the living sacrifice looks like in practice. Holiness is not an abstract concept but a way of life that touches every area of human existence.

Holiness in the Church: Paul immediately turns to the use of spiritual gifts within the body of Christ (Romans 12:3-8). The living sacrifice serves others with the abilities God has given. Whether prophecy or ministry, teaching or exhortation, giving or leading or showing mercy, each gift is to be exercised faithfully for the building up of the body. Holiness is not individualistic piety but active participation in the community of faith.

Holiness in Relationships: Paul then addresses the quality of our relationships (Romans 12:9-16). Love must be "without hypocrisy" (anypokritos, ἀνυπόκριτος), literally "without a mask," genuine and sincere. This love expresses itself in kindness to one another, in honoring others above ourselves, in fervent service to the Lord, in patient endurance of trials, in persistent prayer, in generous sharing with those in need, in hospitality to strangers. It rejoices with those who rejoice and weeps with those who weep. It refuses to be proud but associates with the humble.

> *Greek: anypokritos (ἀνυπόκριτος): without hypocrisy, without a mask, genuine, sincere*

Holiness Toward Enemies: Perhaps the most challenging aspect of the living sacrifice is Paul's instruction regarding enemies (Romans 12:17-21). We are not to repay evil for evil but to pursue what is honorable in the sight of all. As far as it depends on us, we are to live peaceably with everyone. We are not to avenge ourselves but to leave room for God's wrath. If our enemy hungers, we are to feed him; if he thirsts, we are to give him drink. We are not to be overcome by evil but to overcome evil with good.

This teaching echoes the radical ethic of Jesus in the Sermon on the Mount:

> *"But I say to you, love your enemies, bless those who curse you, do good to those who hate you, and pray for those who spitefully use you and persecute you, that you may be sons of your Father in heaven; for He makes His sun rise on the evil and on the good, and sends rain on the just and on the unjust." (Matthew 5:44-45)*

The child of God reflects the character of the Father. God shows kindness to His enemies by providing sun and rain for the righteous and unrighteous alike. We are to do the same, extending grace even to those who wrong us. This is holiness in action: not merely avoiding sin but actively pursuing good, not merely refraining from retaliation but proactively blessing those who harm us.

Holiness in Society: Paul extends the application to civil government (Romans 13:1-7). The living sacrifice respects the authorities God has established, pays taxes honestly, and honors those in positions of responsibility. Christian holiness does not withdraw from society into an isolated enclave but engages responsibly with the structures of human community while maintaining allegiance to a higher King.

Holiness in Personal Conduct: Paul summarizes the ethical demands with a compelling image:

> "The night is far spent, the day is at hand. Therefore let us cast off the works of darkness, and let us put on the armor of light. Let us walk properly, as in the day, not in revelry and drunkenness, not in lewdness and lust, not in strife and envy. But put on the Lord Jesus Christ, and make no provision for the flesh, to fulfill its lusts." (Romans 13:12-14)

The living sacrifice puts on Christ like a garment. His character becomes our clothing. His attitudes become our attitudes. His priorities become our priorities. And we deliberately refuse to make provision for the flesh, cutting off the supply lines that would feed our sinful desires. We do not entertain temptation, do not nurture lusts, do not create opportunities for sin. Instead, we clothe ourselves with Christ and walk in the light of His presence.

V. The Fruit of the Spirit: The Character of Holiness

The apostle Paul provides another perspective on holy living in his letter to the Galatians, where he contrasts the works of the flesh with the fruit of the Spirit.

> "Now the works of the flesh are evident, which are: adultery, fornication, uncleanness, lewdness, idolatry, sorcery, hatred, contentions, jealousies, outbursts of wrath, selfish ambitions, dissensions, heresies, envy, murders, drunkenness, revelries, and the like; of which I tell you beforehand, just as I also told you in time past, that those who practice such things will not inherit the kingdom of God." (Galatians 5:19-21)

This catalogue of vices represents the patterns of the unregenerate life, the life lived according to the flesh. Paul's warning is sobering: those who practice such things will not inherit the kingdom. This does not mean that a single lapse disqualifies a believer, but that a life characterized by such patterns, a life that practices these things as a way of life, is inconsistent with genuine salvation. Those who have been born of the Spirit will produce the fruit of the Spirit.

> *"But the fruit of the Spirit is love, joy, peace, longsuffering, kindness, goodness, faithfulness, gentleness, self-control. Against such there is no law." (Galatians 5:22-23)*

Notice that Paul speaks of "fruit" in the singular, not "fruits." The Spirit produces a unified cluster of character qualities, all of which belong together. Where the Spirit dwells, this fruit will be evident in increasing measure.

Love (agapē, ἀγάπη) heads the list because it is the sum of all Christian virtue. Joy (chara, χαρά) is the deep gladness that transcends circumstances. Peace (eirēnē, εἰρήνη) is the tranquility of soul that comes from reconciliation with God. Longsuffering (makrothymia, μακροθυμία) is patience with difficult people and trying circumstances. Kindness (chrēstotēs, χρηστότης) is gracious benevolence toward others. Goodness (agathōsynē, ἀγαθωσύνη) is moral excellence expressed in generous action. Faithfulness (pistis, πίστις) is reliability and trustworthiness. Gentleness (prautēs, πραΰτης) is meekness, strength under control. Self-control (enkrateia, ἐγκράτεια) is the mastery of one's desires and impulses.

This fruit is not produced by human effort alone but by the indwelling Spirit. Yet we are not passive in its cultivation. Paul concludes:

> *"And those who are Christ's have crucified the flesh with its passions and desires. If we live in the Spirit, let us also walk in the Spirit." (Galatians 5:24-25)*

The crucifixion of the flesh was a decisive action, corresponding to our death with Christ in baptism. The passions and desires of the old nature were nailed to the cross. But we must continue to walk in the Spirit, to keep in step with the Spirit's leading, to cultivate the fruit He produces. Holiness is both a gift received and a discipline practiced.

VI. The Pursuit of Holiness: Practical Disciplines

How do we cultivate this holy life? While transformation is ultimately the Spirit's work, Scripture provides numerous practical disciplines that position us for that work.

The Discipline of Scripture: The word of God is the primary instrument of sanctification. Jesus prayed, "*Sanctify them by Your truth. Your word is truth*" (John 17:17). We have already seen that the mind is renewed through the intake of Scripture. Regular reading, diligent study, careful meditation, and faithful memorization of God's word are essential to holy living.

> *"How can a young man cleanse his way? By taking heed according to Your word. With my whole heart I have sought You; oh, let me not wander from Your commandments! Your word I have hidden in my heart, that I might not sin against You." (Psalm 119:9-11)*

The Discipline of Prayer: Prayer is communion with God, and communion with God transforms us. As we spend time in His presence, His character is impressed upon us. Paul instructed believers to "pray without ceasing" (1 Thessalonians 5:17), to maintain an ongoing attitude of dependence and communion throughout the day. Through prayer we confess our sins, seek forgiveness, and request the power to overcome temptation. Through prayer we align our wills with God's will and receive strength for obedience.

The Discipline of Fellowship: Holiness is not achieved in isolation. We need the encouragement, accountability, and example of fellow believers.

> *"And let us consider one another in order to stir up love and good works, not forsaking the assembling of ourselves together, as is the manner of some, but exhorting one another, and so much the more as you see the Day approaching." (Hebrews 10:24-25)*

We are to "stir up" one another, to provoke one another to love and good works. This requires intentional relationship, honest conversation, and mutual exhortation. Christians who neglect the assembly deprive themselves of essential resources for holy living.

The Discipline of Self-Examination: Paul commanded the Corinthians, "Examine yourselves as to whether you are in the faith. Test yourselves" (2 Corinthians 13:5). Regular self-examination in light of Scripture reveals areas of sin that need to be confessed and forsaken.

> "Search me, O God, and know my heart; try me, and know my anxieties; and see if there is any wicked way in me, and lead me in the way everlasting." (Psalm 139:23-24)

The Discipline of Mortification: Paul used graphic language to describe the ongoing battle against sin: "*Therefore put to death your members which are on the earth: fornication, uncleanness, passion, evil desire, and covetousness, which is idolatry*" (Colossians 3:5).

"Put to death" (nekrōsate, νεκρώσατε) is a violent term. Sin is not merely to be managed but mortified, killed, executed. This requires ruthless honesty about our weaknesses, deliberate avoidance of tempting situations, and immediate action when sin is discovered. We do not negotiate with sin; we put it to death.

Greek: nekrōsate (νεκρώσατε): put to death, mortify, kill

In the Old Testament, the psalmist spoke of worshiping the Lord "in the beauty of holiness" (Psalm 29:2; 96:9). There is a beauty to the holy life that the world cannot comprehend. The world sees holiness as restrictive, joyless, and oppressive. But those who pursue holiness discover that the commands of God are not burdensome but liberating. Sin promises freedom but delivers bondage; holiness promises bondage but delivers freedom.

The prophet Micah summarized what God requires of His people:

> "He has shown you, O man, what is good; and what does the LORD require of you but to do justly, to love mercy, and to walk humbly with your God?" (Micah 6:8)

To do justly, to treat others with fairness and integrity. To love mercy, to extend compassion to the weak and forgiveness to the erring. To walk humbly with God, to live in conscious dependence upon Him, acknowledging our need and His sufficiency. This is the holy life in summary: justice, mercy, and humility before God.

Jesus pronounced blessing upon those who pursue this life: "*Blessed are the pure in heart, for they shall see God*" (Matthew 5:8). The pure heart, the heart cleansed from the pollution of sin and wholly devoted to God, will one day see Him face to face. This is the ultimate goal of holiness: not merely moral improvement in this life but the beatific vision in the life to come.

Until that day, we press on. We present our bodies as living sacrifices. We refuse to be conformed to this world. We allow our minds to be renewed by the word of God. We put off the old man and put on the new. We crucify the flesh and walk in the Spirit. We pursue holiness without which no one will see the Lord.

The grace that saved us is the same grace that sanctifies us. The blood that justified us is the same blood that cleanses us. The Spirit who regenerated us is the same Spirit who transforms us. From first to last, our salvation is the work of God. And yet we work out what God works in, striving to make our calling and election sure, pressing toward the goal for the prize of the upward call of God in Christ Jesus.

Brothers and sisters, let us embrace the call to holiness. Let us offer ourselves fully to the God who has fully given Himself for us. Let us live as those who have been bought with a price, as temples of the Holy Spirit, as priests in His service, as children of the holy God who commands us to be holy as He is holy.

The journey from hearing to believing, from confessing to being baptized, has brought us to this place: the daily walk of the child of God. May we walk worthy of the calling with which we have been called, with all lowliness and gentleness, with longsuffering, bearing with one another in love, endeavoring to keep the unity of the Spirit in the bond of peace. May we grow up in all things into Him who is the head, Christ Himself. And may we one day hear those blessed words: "Well done, good and faithful servant. Enter into the joy of your Lord."

Conclusion
The Door Stands Open

We have come to the end of our journey through God's plan of salvation, but for you, dear reader, this may be just the beginning. We have walked together through the pages of Scripture, tracing the path that leads from spiritual death to eternal life. We have examined the words of prophets and apostles, of Jesus Himself, and we have seen what God requires of those who would be saved. Now the question is no longer what the Bible teaches. The question is what you will do with what you have learned.

I want to speak to you now not as a teacher but as a friend, not as one standing above you but as one kneeling beside you. I have no desire to argue or debate. I simply want to share my heart with you and to extend an invitation that comes not from me but from the Lord Himself.

The Path We Have Traveled

Let us briefly recall the ground we have covered. We began with hearing, for faith comes by hearing, and hearing by the Word of God. We learned that the Hebrew concept of hearing involves far more than sound waves striking the ear. To truly hear God's Word is to receive it with understanding, to attend to it with the heart, to embrace it with the intention to obey. You have heard. The message of the gospel has reached you. The question now is whether you have truly listened.

We then examined faith, that trust in God's promises that transforms the whole person. We discovered that biblical faith is not mere intellectual agreement with certain facts. Even the demons believe that God exists and that Jesus is the Son of God, yet they remain condemned. Saving faith moves beyond the head to grip the heart. It is conviction so deep that it changes how we live. It is confidence so complete that we stake our eternal destiny upon it. Have you believed? Not merely acknowledged, but truly trusted? Have you placed the full weight of your soul upon the promises of God in Christ?

From faith, we turned to repentance, that complete change of mind and direction that marks the transition from the old life to the new. We saw the difference between worldly sorrow, which is merely regret over consequences, and godly sorrow, which grieves over having offended the Holy One. We watched the prodigal son come to himself in the pigpen and make the decision that changed everything: "I will arise and go to my father." Repentance is not just feeling bad about sin; it is turning away from sin and turning toward God. Have you turned? Have you made that decisive break with the old life? Have you set your face toward home?

We considered confession, that public declaration of faith that identifies us with Christ before the world. We learned that to confess is to say the same thing about Jesus that God says, to align our words with divine truth. Confession is faith made audible. It is the overflow of a heart that truly believes. What we believe in secret, we must proclaim in public. The Lord has promised that whoever confesses Him before men, He will confess before the Father in heaven. Have you confessed? Have you declared your allegiance to Jesus Christ? Or does fear of what others might think keep your lips sealed?

We then came to baptism, that burial with Christ in water through which we contact His saving blood and rise to walk in newness of life. We traced the rich Old Testament background of water and salvation: Noah saved through the flood, Israel delivered through the sea, Naaman cleansed in the Jordan. We saw that baptism is not an optional extra for those already saved but the divinely appointed means through which the penitent believer receives the remission of sins. In baptism, we are united with Christ in His death, burial, and resurrection. We die to the old life and rise to the new. Have you been baptized? Have you been buried with Christ and raised to walk in newness of life?

Finally, we explored what it means to live as children of God. Salvation is not merely a moment but a journey. We are called to present our bodies as living sacrifices, to be transformed by the renewing of our minds, to walk in holiness without which no one will see the Lord. The same grace that saves us also sanctifies us. The Christian life is a daily walk with Christ, growing in His likeness, bearing the fruit of His Spirit, pressing on toward the goal. If you have obeyed the gospel, this beautiful journey lies before you. If you have not, this is what awaits you on the other side of obedience.

A Personal Word

I do not know your story. I do not know what has brought you to this point in your life or what obstacles stand between you and faith. Perhaps you were raised in a religious home but never made a personal commitment to Christ. Perhaps you have been far from God for many years and wonder if He would even receive you now. Perhaps you have been hurt by religious people and are suspicious of anyone who claims to speak for God. Perhaps you have intellectual questions that remain unanswered, doubts that trouble your mind in the quiet hours. Perhaps you are simply afraid of what commitment to Christ might cost you.

Whatever your situation, I want you to know that God understands. He knows your heart better than you know it yourself. He sees your struggles, your fears, your doubts, your wounds. And He loves you. Not because you deserve it, for none of us do. Not because you have earned it, for salvation cannot be earned. He loves you because that is who He is. God is love, and He demonstrated that love by sending His Son to die for you while you were still a sinner, while you were still His enemy, while you wanted nothing to do with Him. That is the kind of God we are talking about. That is the Father who waits for prodigals to come home.

I also want you to know that I am not asking you to do something I have not done myself. I have heard the gospel and believed it. I have repented of my sins. I have confessed Jesus as Lord. I have been buried with Him in baptism and raised to walk in newness of life. And I am still walking, still stumbling sometimes, still getting back up, still depending every day on the grace that saved me. I am not a perfect Christian. I am simply a forgiven one. And what God has done for me, He will do for you.

The Invitation

So here is my invitation, or rather, here is God's invitation through me: Come.

Come to the One who said, "Come to Me, all you who labor and are heavy laden, and I will give you rest." Come to the One who promised, "The one who comes to Me I will by no means cast out." Come to the One who declared, "I am the way, the truth, and the life. No one comes to the Father except through Me." Jesus is not one path among many; He is the only path. He is not a good teacher among good teachers; He is the Son of the living God. And He is calling you to Himself.

Do not let fear hold you back. Yes, following Christ will cost you something. It may cost you relationships, reputation, comfort, ambition. But what does it profit a man to gain the whole world and lose his own soul? Whatever you give up for Christ, you will receive back a hundredfold, both in this life and in the life to come. The temporary sacrifices of discipleship are nothing compared to the eternal weight of glory that awaits those who endure.

Do not let doubt hold you back. You do not need to have every question answered before you can believe. Faith is not the absence of questions; it is trust in the midst of questions. The father who brought his demon-possessed son to Jesus cried out with tears, "Lord, I believe; help my unbelief!" Jesus did not reject him for his doubts. He healed his son. Bring your doubts to Jesus. He is not threatened by your questions. He is big enough to handle your uncertainties.

Do not let your past hold you back. There is no sin so great that the blood of Christ cannot cleanse it. There is no life so broken that the grace of God cannot restore it. Paul persecuted the church and consented to the death of Christians, yet he became an apostle. Peter denied the Lord three times, yet he preached the first gospel sermon. The woman at the well had been married five times and was living with a man who was not her husband, yet she became an evangelist to her whole village. Your past does not disqualify you from grace; your past is precisely why you need grace.

Do not let delay hold you back. Tomorrow is promised to no one. The Scripture says, "Today, if you will hear His voice, do not harden your hearts." Every day that passes with the gospel rejected is another day of walking toward judgment instead of toward life. Felix told Paul, "When I have a convenient time I will call for you." As far as we know, that convenient time never came. Do not make the same tragic mistake. Now is the accepted time. Now is the day of salvation.

What Will You Do?

I cannot make this decision for you. No one can. It must be your choice, your faith, your commitment. But I can tell you what awaits you if you will respond.

If you will believe in Jesus Christ as the Son of God, trusting Him with your whole heart, you will have taken the first step toward life.

If you will repent of your sins, turning away from the old life and turning toward God, you will find that He is already running to meet you.

If you will confess Jesus as Lord, declaring before others that you belong to Him, you will discover that He is not ashamed to call you His own.

If you will be baptized for the remission of your sins, buried with Christ in water and raised to walk in newness of life, you will rise from that water a new creation. The old will have passed away. The new will have come.

And if you will walk in holiness, offering yourself as a living sacrifice, you will experience the abundant life that Jesus promised, a life of purpose and meaning, of peace and joy, of hope that does not disappoint.

This is not a religion of burdens and restrictions. This is freedom. This is life. This is coming home.

A Final Word

If you are ready to respond, I urge you to find a faithful church that teaches the Word of God and to speak with the minister or elders there. Tell them that you want to obey the gospel. They will rejoice with you and help you take the steps we have discussed in this book. Do not try to walk this path alone. God has given us the church, the body of Christ, to encourage us, support us, and walk alongside us.

If you are not yet ready, I understand. But I ask you not to set this book aside and forget what you have read. Keep thinking. Keep searching. Keep asking questions. And keep your heart open to the possibility that what you have read is true. God is patient, and He will continue to pursue you with His love. But do not presume upon His patience forever. The door of mercy stands open today, but it will not stand open forever.

Whatever you decide, know that you have been in my prayers as I have written these words. I have prayed for every person who would read this book, that God would open hearts and illumine minds, that His Spirit would convict of sin and draw souls to Christ. I have prayed for you. And I will continue to pray that you will find the salvation that God offers so freely and so lovingly.

"Behold, I stand at the door and knock. If anyone hears My voice and opens the door, I will come in to him and dine with him, and he with Me." (Revelation 3:20, NKJV)

He is standing at the door. He is knocking. Will you open?

May the grace of the Lord Jesus Christ, and the love of God, and the fellowship of the Holy Spirit be with you.

Recommended Resources

The thoughts contained in this book did not emerge in isolation. Over many years of study, certain works have shaped my understanding of Scripture and deepened my appreciation for God's plan of salvation. I offer these recommendations not as required reading but as companions for your own journey. Each has blessed me, and I trust they will bless you as well.

This is not an exhaustive list, nor do I endorse every word in every volume. Read with discernment, as the Bereans did, testing all things against the Scriptures. But read. The Christian life is a learning life, and there is always more to discover about the depths of God's grace.

On Salvation

K.C. Moser, *The Gist of Romans*

A classic work from the restoration movement that illuminates the relationship between grace and faith in Paul's great epistle. Moser writes with clarity and conviction.

Jimmy Allen, *Re-Baptism? What One Must Know to Be Born Again*

A careful examination of what Scripture teaches about the new birth, written with pastoral sensitivity for those wrestling with questions about their own conversion.

T.W. Brents, *The Gospel Plan of Salvation*

A thorough and systematic treatment of God's plan of redemption. Though written in an earlier era, its biblical arguments remain compelling and relevant.

On Baptism

Jack Cottrell, *Baptism: A Biblical Study*

A comprehensive examination of baptism's meaning, mode, and purpose. Cottrell handles the biblical text carefully and addresses common objections thoughtfully.

Everett Ferguson, *Baptism in the Early Church*

A scholarly work tracing baptismal practice through the first five centuries of Christianity. Ferguson demonstrates that immersion for the remission of sins was the universal practice of the early church.

G.R. Beasley-Murray, *Baptism in the New Testament*

A landmark study by a Baptist scholar whose careful examination of Scripture led him to affirm baptism's essential role in salvation. His honesty with the text is refreshing.

On Holy Living

Jerry Bridges, *The Pursuit of Holiness*

A practical and convicting guide to sanctification. Bridges writes as one who has walked the path and knows both its difficulties and its rewards.

J.C. Ryle, *Holiness: Its Nature, Hindrances, Difficulties, and Roots*

A classic work by the nineteenth-century bishop that has lost none of its power. Ryle's call to holiness is urgent, biblical, and deeply pastoral.

Word Study Tools

W.E. Vine, *Vine's Complete Expository Dictionary of Old and New Testament Words*

An accessible guide to the original languages for readers without formal training in Hebrew and Greek. Invaluable for personal Bible study.

Spiros Zodhiates, *The Complete Word Study Dictionary: New Testament*

A more detailed resource for those who wish to go deeper into the Greek text. Zodhiates provides thorough definitions and theological insights.

Above all, I commend to you the Book of books. No commentary can replace the Scriptures themselves. Read them daily. Meditate on them continually. Let them dwell in you richly. For in them you have the very words of eternal life.

Made in the USA
Coppell, TX
14 February 2026

71321160R00066